The Parenthood Decision

Beverly Engel

The Parenthood Decision

Deciding Whether You
Are Ready and Willing
to Become a Parent

MAIN STREET BOOKS
Doubleday
New York London Toronto Sydney Auckland

A Main Street Book
PUBLISHED BY DOUBLEDAY
a division of Bantam Doubleday Dell Publishing Group, Inc.
1540 Broadway, New York, New York 10036

Main Street Books, Doubleday, and the portrayal of a building with a tree
are trademarks of Doubleday, a division of Bantam Doubleday Dell Publishing
Group, Inc.

Library of Congress Cataloging-in-Publication Data

Engel, Beverly.
The parenthood decision : deciding whether you are ready and
willing to become a parent / Beverly Engel.
    p.   cm.
Includes bibliographical references.
1. Parenting.   I. Title.
HQ755.8.E524   1998
649′.1—dc21   98-13932
CIP

ISBN 0-385-48980-3
June 1998
First Edition

10   9   8   7   6   5   4   3   2   1

To my dear friends Patti McDermott, Connie Davidson, and Honey Burns—three of the best parents I've ever known.

Acknowledgments

First and foremost, I wish to thank Nancy Love, my agent, for her constant support and tireless efforts on my part. I also wish to thank Frances Jones at Doubleday for helping to make this a better book with her excellent editing. And finally, much appreciation to all the parents and would-be parents who were interviewed for the book or agreed to have their stories told in an effort to help potential parents everywhere to make this important decision.

Contents

Introduction

HAVING A BABY has become an increasingly popular idea, causing thousands of couples and singles alike to contemplate parenthood. Despite their desire to become parents, many of these people have deep concerns about whether they are prepared at this time for the long-term commitment or whether they will make good parents. If you are one of these people, *The Parenthood Decision* will help you to make a decision that you will be comfortable with for the rest of your life.

Deciding whether or not to become a parent may very well be the most important decision you will make in your life. While the decisions concerning marriage and career are also important ones and certainly impact one's life, those decisions can be reversed. Although marriage is supposed to be a lifelong commitment, in actuality, it doesn't always work out that way. And while most people choose a career with the idea that they will stay in it a lifetime (especially when there are years of education and/or training involved), we are also seeing that people now change careers at least once and often several times in their lifetime.

But the decision to have a baby (or adopt a child) is *not* reversible. The decision to become a parent involves another person's entire life. Becoming a parent means you are ultimately responsible for another human being's emotional and physical well-being and, in a very real sense, their very life. Your infant will be totally dependent on you for food, shelter, protection, and nurturing. Your toddler will need you to teach him or her about love, danger, boundaries, and limits. And your school-age child will depend on you for lessons about socializing with others, respecting the property and rights of others, as well as taking risks and saying no. Whether your child grows up to be a confident, self-assured person capable of respecting and loving other people will, for the most part, be totally up to you.

If what I am saying sounds overly dramatic or frightening, I am sorry. But it is my goal to encourage each person reading this book to take the parenthood decision very seriously. To this end, I will present invaluable information that will help you make the right decision—for yourself, your mate (if you have one), and most important, for the child you are thinking about having.

Although, ultimately, you and you alone will have to make this decision, no one should have to do so in a vacuum. I will act as your guide through the maze of questions, concerns, and conflicts that you will inevitably encounter as you begin to seriously focus on this momentous decision. The questions and issues I bring up will often help clear up some of your confusion. At other times, I will present issues for you to consider that will cause you to feel even more confused— create even more internal conflict. Although it won't feel like it at the time, you will find this too will ultimately help you in your decision.

Many of you are reading this book because you are already aware of what a tremendous responsibility becoming a parent is, and some of you are already aware of the potential problems that might prevent you from being a good parent. If this is your situation, I wish to commend you for acting responsibly. Admitting your fears and shortcomings now can be the first step to overcoming them and is in itself an indication that you have the potential to be a responsible, loving parent. I encourage you to continue to be honest about your fears as you read the book. Sometimes fears are only indicators of insecurity—other times they are warnings. By the time you've completed this book and worked on the issues presented to you, I am confident you will be able to make the distinction.

My reasons for writing this book are numerous. My primary reason is that in the course of my twenty-four-year career as a marriage, family, and child counselor, I have worked with many couples who have had difficulties with the parenting process. They came to my office totally overwhelmed and often on the brink of divorce due to the stresses of raising a child. Many of these clients told me they had been pressured by either their mate, their families, or their friends to have a child and that they wished they had never allowed the pressure to get to them. Many had realized, unfortunately too late, that they were not good parents, either because of their personality, their background, or the fact that they did not have a good relationship with their mate.

As an expert in working with adult victims of emotional, physical, and sexual abuse, I also felt it was important to educate those who had the potential to become abusive or neglectful parents about the pressures of having children. At the same time, I wanted to reassure those who had less than happy childhoods themselves that not all abused or neglected children become abusive parents.

I found that a vast majority of my clients who had been abused or neglected as children were afraid they would repeat the cycle of abuse if they were to become parents. Therefore, I felt it was important to explain the effects abuse and neglect can have on potential parents, to educate potential parents on what it takes to be a good parent and present a way for them to explore how they might react in various circumstances.

At the same time, many of my single clients were coming in telling me they were tired of waiting until they met the right partner to have a child. Some of these clients were women in their late thirties and early forties who were feeling the pressure of their biological clocks, some were lesbian and gay clients who had always wanted to be parents, and a few were single men. All wanted to explore the possibility of becoming a single parent and to be made aware of the potential problems that lie ahead for them.

I too was going through my own conflicts about never having become a mother. Although I had determined many years before not to have children, recognizing that my own abusive childhood had created a personality that was not suitable for the parenting role, I had healed a great deal and began to wonder whether I had changed enough to now be a good parent. At the age of forty, I suddenly started feeling maternal stirrings, as many baby boomers and late bloomers were. For quite some time, I dismissed these feelings, telling myself that it was definitely too late for me to become a mother. But the feelings continued to plague me. Eventually, I gave into them. While I didn't wish to become pregnant, nor to adopt an infant, I did seriously consider adopting an older child. To this end, I began searching in libraries and bookstores for books on helping potential parents decide if they were emotionally prepared to have a child.

It turned out that there had been several books written on the parenthood decision, most notably *The Baby Decision: How to Make the Most Important Choice of Your Life* by Merle Bombardieri and *Children: To Have or Have Not?* by Diane Elvenstar. While there was some important information in these books, they were quite outdated (both being over ten years old) and didn't include information for single parents. More importantly, they didn't delve into the factor of emotional readiness deeply enough.

I did find a book written specifically for single women, entitled *Single Mothers by Choice: A Guidebook for Single Women Who Are Considering or Have Chosen Motherhood* by Jane Mattes. While the title implies that the book will help single women make this important decision, there are only a few pages at the beginning of the book offering this kind of advice and it isn't very comprehensive. The book is primarily for women who have already made their decision. It helps women decide whether they want to conceive the child themselves or adopt and discusses the legal and moral aspects of being a single mother. While I began to recommend this book to my single female clients who had already decided to have a baby, I could find no book available to help them make their decision.

Although obviously written specifically for couples, *The Transition to Parenthood: How a First Child Changes a Marriage* by Jay Belsky, Ph.D., and John Kelly was more of what I was looking for concerning emotional readiness. Based on what is referred to as a landmark study, the authors traced the lives of three couples, showing how their first child affected their marriage. While it presents important information, particularly in specifying the types of couples who continue to make their relationship work, it did not make any suggestions to potential parents or guide them to discover on their own whether they are ready for parenthood.

And so, as is often the case with me, I was left to develop my own process of discovering whether I was emotionally prepared for parenthood, which ultimately became the seeds for this book. I went through a process similar to the one I am now presenting here—examining my reasons for wanting a child, becoming more educated about what having a child entails, closely examining my lifestyle to determine whether it was conducive to parenting, and finally, undergoing a complete self-analysis to determine whether, in fact, I was able to be a good parent.

I ultimately decided against adopting a child because, at the time, I had a full practice and was working long hours four days a week. Most of my clients needed to come to sessions in the evening, so I often worked as late as ten o'clock in the evening. Also, because my work was sometimes stressful and I was so dedicated to my clients, I feared I wouldn't have the emotional energy to devote to a child. I was grateful, though, that I was able to put the idea to rest once and for all and equally grateful for the process I had developed. I hope by reading this book, you too will be able to decide whether you should become a parent.

Author's Note

The sources for the information in the book are as follows: relevant research studies, case examples from my twenty-four years as a psychotherapist, anecdotal information from potential parents, and interviews from potential as well as actual parents.

Please note that the information in this book applies to all those contemplating becoming parents—couples, single women, and single men. While I most often use the words "marriage" and "husband and wife," I am referring to all couples, whether married, living together, gay, or lesbian.

Also note that for purposes of simplicity and clarity, I most often use the phrase "having a baby," even though the book is for those who are considering adopting a baby or an older child as well as for those contemplating giving birth to a baby.

Part I

The Parenthood Decision

ONE

Why You May Need Help Making the Parenthood Decision

IN SPITE of the fact that the idea of parenthood is becoming increasingly enticing to many people and more and more are contemplating taking the big step, parenthood also poses some serious concerns. Most people are smart enough to realize that just *wanting* a baby doesn't mean one is physically, mentally, and emotionally prepared to *have* one. Nor does the desire to have a baby mean that one will necessarily be a good parent. Many potential parents are plagued with questions and doubts such as: "Am I ready to become a parent?" "How will having a baby affect my marriage . . . my career?" "Will I make a good parent?"

Nowadays, more than ever, we are keenly aware of the fact that some people make better parents than others. With child abuse, delinquency, and runaways at a record high and with our growing awareness as to what contributes to these problems, people are more cautious about having children than they have ever been before.

And with the stresses of modern living and the plethora of social and political problems we face, many potential parents are uncertain whether they have the time, strength, or patience to raise children or whether they want to bring children into this chaotic world.

In addition, many potential parents are stopped by their fears—fear of childbirth, fear of losing their identity, fear of losing their attractiveness, fear of losing their personal free time or their alone time with their partner.

Many are certain they want children but are not sure that now is the time. For various reasons (problems in their relationship, career pressures), they may feel they should wait. At the same time, they may feel compelled to have a baby now. They may feel pressured by their biological clock, by well-meaning relatives or friends, or by a strong desire for parenthood.

If you relate to any of the above situations, this book will help you resolve your conflicts about this major decision. By presenting important information, providing exercises, and posing thought-provoking questions, I will help both those who are unclear whether this is the right time to become a parent and those who are undecided whether parenthood is right for them.

In addition to addressing the concerns and ambivalence of couples, *The Parenthood Decision* also addresses those of single women who are considering becoming parents. Many women, discouraged about ever meeting a man they will want to marry, much less a man they would want to be the father to their baby, are seriously considering becoming single mothers. For example, the U.S. Census Bureau reported in 1995 that more than a quarter of the nation's never-married women now become mothers, an increase of 70 percent in the last decade.

The increase was particularly sharp among educated and professional women. The number of single women who have become mothers is actually higher when you take into consideration that the census report only counted never-married mothers, leaving out the many divorced and widowed women who went on to have children after their marriages ended. With celebrities like Michelle Pfeiffer, Rosie O'Donnell, Madonna, and Kate Jackson becoming single mothers, this trend will no doubt increase.

And it isn't only women who are longing for a child. Since fatherhood has finally been given the focus and respect it so richly deserves, today there are a growing number of men who are also yearning for parenthood. As never before, men are trying to reconcile deeply ingrained notions about marital roles and high-powered careers with equally strong needs to nurture and bond. Single men are also considering parenthood in numbers unheard of just a few years ago. Some are considering adopting; others are asking female friends to have their baby.

Last but not least, today more and more teenagers are wanting to have a baby. Often motivated by a desire to have someone to love or to hold on to a boyfriend, these young women openly talk about their desire for a child. While these teenagers are not likely to buy the book, I strongly recommend that their parents, teachers, and other concerned adults do and that they share the information with the teenager.

There are also a great many women and teens who are already pregnant but are undecided whether to keep their baby or give it up for adoption. If this applies to you, this book will help you with your feelings of ambivalence whether they are centered around not being certain you can adequately take care of a child at this time, not being sure whether you will be a good parent, or, for those of you who are in a relationship, not being clear as to whether your relationship can withstand the added stress of having a child.

Whatever your situation, *The Parenthood Decision* will help you take a close and honest look at your life to determine whether parenthood is right for you. It will help you make your decision whether you are in a relationship or not, whether you are a potential father or a potential mother, whether you are planning to give birth to a baby or adopt a child. It will, in short, help anyone considering bringing a child into their home and heart.

In addition to helping those who are ambivalent concerning the prospect of parenthood, *The Parenthood Decision* is also for all those couples and singles who have already decided to get pregnant or plan to adopt. Many potential parents plan for a baby for several years, putting aside a portion of their earnings, buying a house in a neighborhood within a good school district, sometimes even changing jobs or careers in order to have a more flexible schedule. But most people do not prepare *emotionally* for parenthood.

Unfortunately, there is little help available to guide potential parents with the emotional aspects of this decision, either from their families, in school, or in the media. Some people have suggested we should be issued a license before being allowed to become a parent or at the very least be required to take a course in parenting. While you may feel these measures are too extreme, no one can argue that the more one knows about him or herself before deciding to have a child, the better parent one is likely to be.

The basic premise of *The Parenthood Decision* is that potential parents should be physically, mentally, and emotionally prepared to have a child. This involves taking a look at one's present situation—career, relationship, financial status, health. It involves becoming educated about what parenthood requires and what it entails. And last but not least, it involves taking a close look at one's personality and the personality of one's partner.

I will help you as potential parents to explore all aspects of parenthood, from whether you have the kind of personality that is conducive to parenting, to whether you are willing to give up or postpone some of your career and other goals in order to focus on raising an emotionally healthy child. I will help single parents decide whether they can handle the stress and responsibility of parenthood alone and help couples decide whether their relationship can withstand the added stress and pressures of parenthood.

There are many aspects of the parenthood decision. And while it is impossible to address them all, I have designed *The Parenthood Decision* to help potential parents explore three major areas:

1. Whether you are physically, mentally, and emotionally *ready* to become a parent at this time

2. Whether you are *willing* to face the changes in your lifestyle and relationship that this lifelong commitment entails

3. Whether you are emotionally *able* to provide the kind of environment necessary to raise a healthy child

Part I will address the parenthood decision in general, including such issues as exploring your reasons for wanting a child and avoiding the most common mistakes potential parents make when deciding and dealing with ambivalence.

In Part II, I address whether you are *ready* to become a parent. In addition to offering important information on what it means to be prepared for a baby and how having a baby will affect your life, I will offer questions and exercises that will test your readiness and help you decide whether you are prepared to become a parent at this time.

In Part III, I will address whether you are *willing* to be a parent at this time. While you may believe you are willing, you may not have all the facts. By providing important information about what being a parent actually entails, I hope to help you look clearly at the day-to-day realities of parenting. I will again provide exercises and questions to help you focus on this issue in ways that you may have overlooked or to look at it from an entirely different perspective.

While you may have determined that you are indeed ready and willing to have a baby, you may not be sure you are *able* to be a good parent. Many potential parents are plagued with questions such as: "Will I repeat the same mistakes my parents made?" "Will I be a better parent than mine were to me?" "Will I have the patience, tolerance, and stamina necessary to be a good parent?" Consequently, in Part IV, I will help you answer these questions by providing important information and questions aimed at revealing your innermost thoughts and feelings, as well as exercises to help you get to know yourself better as a potential parent.

Throughout the book, I encourage you to take your time in answering the questions I pose and to answer them as honestly as possible. Try to remain open to learning about yourself (and your partner) without becoming overly critical. Your feelings will no doubt vacillate as you discover more and more about yourself and/or your partner, but I encourage you to read the book through completely and to answer all the questions before making any decision. It isn't unusual for potential parents to change their minds several times during the decision-making process before reaching their final decision. This does not mean they are indecisive people. In fact, the more you allow yourself to go through a variety of emotions, the more certain you will be about your final decision, since you will have examined your feelings from different points of view.

When you have completed the first four parts of the book, you will have a more comprehensive picture of yourself as a potential parent and will be able to make your decision from a place of confidence.

It may be that you discover you are ready, willing, and able to become a parent and that a celebration is in order. Or it may be that you decide that you are willing and able to become a good parent, but you are not quite ready for the responsibility. Or you may realize that while you are ready and willing, you will need to do some work on yourself or your relationship before you will be able to parent in the way you want.

Therefore, I offer one last part to the book, Part V: If You Are Not Ready, Willing, or Able. For those who still have the hope of becoming a parent, I will make suggestions as to how you can remedy the situation—whatever it might be— that prevents you from being ready at this time. For those of you who have decided it would be best if you didn't become a parent at all, I will offer hope and alternatives.

At the end of the book, a Bibliography, a recommended reading list for further information on specific issues, and a list of resources have been provided.

Becoming a parent can be the most rewarding, fulfilling act of one's life. Through our children we can experience compassion, learn patience and tolerance, and experience a depth of love we aren't likely to feel any other way. At the same time, parenthood can also be the most stressful, demanding endeavor we will ever undertake. Being prepared, especially being emotionally prepared for a child, will help potential parents feel confident about their ability to be the best parent they can be.

TWO

Exploring Your Reasons
for Wanting a Child

ONE OF the most important aspects of your decision and the
obvious place to begin is by looking carefully at your reasons
for wanting a child at this time. While it may seem as if the
reasons are obvious, after some serious soul-searching, you
may discover reasons you were unaware of. The following exercise is a beginning point from which to start.

EXERCISE: Why Do You Want a Child?

1. List all the reasons that come to mind for wanting to
have a child. Don't think too much about it. Just write. Be
careful not to censor yourself; no one else need see this list but
you.

2. Now read your list over carefully, paying close attention to how you feel about each of your responses. Do you feel

your reasons are valid and positive? Or are you ashamed of some of them?

This list more than likely reveals how you really feel, before you are influenced by what I am about to present. It will be important information for you to refer to later on as you read the book.

Some of you may not be too sure why you want a child or may question what your real motives are. If this is the case, the following questions may provide some answers.

Questions: Discovering Your Real Reasons for Wanting a Child

1. How would you describe your life now? Happy? Fulfilling? Average? Empty? Stressful? Unhappy?

2. How would you describe your relationship with your partner?

3. How do you feel about your work? Is it "just a job" or a career?

4. How do you imagine having a child will affect your life?

5. Do you imagine having a child would make you feel more accepted, more included in life? Why?

6. Do you feel you will be incomplete if you do not have a child? Why?

7. Do you feel you aren't a "real" woman or man if you do not reproduce? Why?

8. If you are unable to have children, would adopting also make you feel like a "real" woman or man? Why?

9. Do you think your parents will treat you with greater respect if you had a child?

10. Do you think your boss, friends, and neighbors will regard you differently if you have a child?

11. Do you want a child because you are lonely or unhappy? Do you expect a child will change these feelings?

12. If you do expect a child to make you happier, why will this happen?

13. Do you want a child to be there to take care of you when you are sick or old?

Why Do We Want Children?

Our ideas and images about parenthood are formed long before we begin considering having a child. From the time girls become aware that the sexes are different, they learn that having babies is something that many women do. Socialization continues to reinforce the message throughout childhood and into adulthood. Girls are continuously prepared to become nurturers, first by being given baby dolls, later on by encouraging them (or, in some cases, requiring them) to take care of other people's children. Before long, even very young girls begin to think about having children of their own.

While male children are not socialized to nurture, they are taught at an early age that males grow up to be "daddies" and they too learn that one day they will grow up to have their own children.

These early experiences are extremely powerful. Despite the fact that women today have a choice whether to have children or not, only a small number who are married and of childbearing age remain voluntarily childless. Most women and most men expect to have children. More important, most people *want* to have them.

Although early socialization is a major motivating factor for wanting children, each individual and each couple have different reasons for wanting children at any given time.

In *The Motherhood Report: How Women Feel About Being Mothers* by Louis Genevie, Ph.D., and Eva Margolies, the authors surveyed 1,100 mothers between the ages of eighteen and eighty throughout the United States. When asked why they decided to become parents, nine out of ten women gave the reasons: "I love children" and "I wanted a close family." "I wanted someone to love" was cited as important by three out of four.

These answers are consistent with the conditioning women receive to become nurturers. But the survey also found other expectations which were inconsistent with the notion that women want children because they want to nurture. On a deeper level, the desire to have a child was often less a desire to nurture than to be nurtured.

All too often, when talking to clients about their reasons for wanting a child I hear, "I want someone who will love me unconditionally, someone who will always be there for me." This was the case with my client Judith:

"I realize now that the reason I wanted a baby was to get the love I didn't receive from my own mother. My mother was cold and distant and seldom showed me any affection. All during my childhood, I yearned to be held and cuddled like I saw other parents doing with their kids. As an adult, I still craved physical attention, which I looked to sex to fill. But nothing filled the empty feeling inside me; nothing satisfied the craving. Somehow I convinced myself that having a baby would do it. That a baby would give me what no one else had."

This is also often the underlying reason many men have for wanting a child. For many, the prospect of parenthood represents the chance to relive their childhood in a happier, more perfect way. Unfortunately, this desire leads most potential parents to envision parenthood in an idealistic, often unrealistic way. Having a child, no matter how good an experience it may turn out to be, cannot erase the negative, unhappy childhood that you may have experienced. In addition, it is too much of a burden to put on your child.

Questionable Reasons for Wanting a Child

In addition to wanting a child in order to somehow undo negative aspects of your own childhood or to give you someone who will love you unconditionally to make up for not feeling loved by your own parents, there are many other questionable reasons for wanting a child. I use the word "questionable," as opposed to "unacceptable" or "negative," because we are not talking about black and white here. You aren't *wrong* for having any of the following reasons for wanting a child. The important thing is to look closely at your feelings and acknowledge that some may lead to questionable motivations for having children—motivations that should be acknowledged and dealt with prior to making the decision to become a parent.

• **"I love the idea of pregnancy, creating another life from my own body."**

Many women give this as their reason for wanting to have a baby and this is certainly a natural desire. After all, women's bodies are created in such a way as to encourage this desire. We even have what is commonly called a "biological clock," our bodies' way of encouraging us to have babies by stimulating certain hormones. But these physical signals and the emotional desire to procreate that go with them are not a good enough reason to seriously consider becoming pregnant. Becoming a parent is far more than giving birth. As I stated earlier, it is a lifetime responsibility and commitment.

Rachel discovered this, unfortunately, only after she had already had her son Thomas. By the time Thomas was two years old, Rachel found that she no longer saw motherhood in such a positive light.

"I realize now that I was in love with the *idea* of giving birth. It felt like such a miracle, to actually create another human being from your own body. It made me feel incredibly powerful. But I was totally unprepared for the responsibility of it and it turned out to be too much for me. I began to feel trapped and I just couldn't handle the constant pressure to take care of his needs. I started becoming enraged with him over the slightest thing, like if he spilled his milk. I was afraid I was going to really hurt him one day. Finally, in desperation, I gave him to my mother to raise."

- **"Having a baby will bring us closer together."**

Although this is one of the most questionable reasons to bring a child into the world, it is one of the most common reasons couples give. Over the years, I have counseled dozens of couples who thought that starting a family would save their marriage. But I, like most marriage counselors and psychologists, always advise couples that this is not a good reason to have a child. First of all, it is a terribly heavy burden to place on a child. Second, a shaky marriage or relationship is not the best environment in which to raise a child. If the marriage or relationship doesn't get better, one or both of you may end up taking out your anger and frustration on the child. It isn't fair to the child to bring her or him into a situation where there is tension or fighting or where he or she will have to go through a separation or divorce.

It's understandable that you want to believe that a baby might provide the glue that can hold a shaky relationship together, that having a child might give you a common purpose. But a baby does little to cement a questionable marriage. In fact, it usually adds to the stress and difficulties that already exist.

- **"Time's running out. If I'm going to have a baby, it better be now."**

Both men and women suffer from the fear of growing too old to have children, but it is women who feel the most pressure from their biological clocks. The phenomenon of the "biological clock" is a fairly new one, rearing its head about 1980 or so. In our mother's day, women tended to get pregnant soon after they got married unless they couldn't have a child. But today women typically put off childbearing for a number of years after marriage in order to pursue higher education and career or other goals. Before they know it, they are in their late thirties and time is running out.

The problem is, many women become so focused on their biological clock that they don't take the time to figure out whether they really *want* to have children or not. The mere fact that they may not be *able* to have a child if they don't act soon may completely cloud the issue.

Before you have a child based on your fear of time running out, consider this question. If you haven't truly wanted a baby enough in the past twenty or so years to make room for it in your life, why do you suddenly want it now? Did you always want to have children but somehow didn't know it or did you just notice you wanted them when "time was running out"?

It is becoming more and more common for both women and men to have children later in life. Chances are, when you are truly ready to have a child, you will manage to do it one way or another, even if it means adopting.

• **"My parents want grandchildren."**

My client Tina, a twenty-nine-year-old architect who is married to a doctor, surprised me one day by telling me that she was seriously thinking about having a baby. The reason I was so surprised was that she'd always been so adamant about not having children.

"It's because my parents want grandchildren more than anything else in the world. I love them so much; they've been so good to me . . . They tell me that once I become a mother

I'll love it. That it's natural to hesitate, to resist being a parent because you have to give up so much. But they say the rewards more than make up for the sacrifices. It sure seemed to be the case for them."

I was also surprised to hear that Tina's parents were exerting so much pressure on her about getting pregnant, since she had always described them as parents who had allowed her to make her own decisions in the past.

"It surprised me too. They certainly aren't the typical 'grandparents' type. I mean, they're still very active and my mother looks like she's still in her forties. They certainly aren't ready for the rocking chair."

Some parents, like Tina's, believe that if they don't "encourage" their children to have babies, their children may end up never having any. They believe it's a parent's obligation to help one's children see the benefits of being a parent. But this is not the case. It's not a parent's responsibility, obligation, or right to try to influence their adult children's decisions about procreation. Ideally, a parent's role should be to remain neutral about the issue, allowing each child the room and acceptance to make a wise decision based on their needs, their situation, and their personal values. While it's fine to point out the benefits of parenting, generally those who came from a relatively happy and reasonably functional home life recognize the benefits on their own.

Some people are simply unwilling to abdicate their own life and interests in order to devote themselves to having children and this was the case with Tina. Instead of buckling under the pressure from her parents, she was finally able to tell them that while she appreciated their desire for grandchildren, she had to live her life her own way, and that was without children, at least for the time being.

Another way of thinking about this is that if you are unwilling or unable to say no to Mom and Dad, you certainly aren't ready for the responsibilities of parenthood.

• **"Everyone else is doing it. I feel left out."**

If people you admire are having children—whether it is friends, family, or celebrities—it's understandable that this will influence you. But doing something just because everyone else is doing it is not the best reason for having a child.

It is difficult to resist the pressure to have a baby when one's own peers, family, and friends begin having children. The urge to join in can be overwhelming, as it was with Sylvia and Eddie.

"Before we got married, we discussed whether or not we were going to have kids. I felt strongly about not having kids because of the way I was raised and I wanted to avoid future problems if Sylvia wanted them. But she agreed. She'd come from a very large family where she had to fight for any little bit of attention she got from her parents and liked the idea of the two of us devoting our lives to one another.

"Then after we'd been happily married for six years, Sylvia's best friend had a baby. A year later, a close colleague at work had one. Suddenly it seemed to her that everyone had a baby but her and she felt left out. She told me she no longer felt like she had anything in common with her closest friends because they were all focused on their kids. She started pressuring me to have a child. I still feel the way I've always felt and so we fight about it all the time now. And frankly, I'm not even sure she really wants a baby or if she's being influenced by the current 'baby craze.' "

It is difficult to distinguish between internal and external pressures. It is a common psychological process to take the ideas and values of others and make them our own (a process known as "internalization"). The problem arises when we un-consciously internalize pressures and trends and begin to believe they are what we wanted all along. When the desire to have a baby comes not from your own heart and soul, after much thought and deliberation, but suddenly seems to be what you wanted "all along," it may be in response to outside pressures and societal attitudes.

- **"I want to be treated like I'm special. Like I really matter."**

All but the very young would be embarrassed to tell anyone about this motive for having a baby, but it is surprising how many women have a baby for this very reason.

Some realized it at the time, on a conscious level, like my twenty-two-year-old client Susan:

"I liked all the attention I saw my friends getting when they were pregnant. Everyone treated them so great, like they were special or something. Like men pulling out their chairs and getting up to give them their seat, that kind of thing. Everyone ignored me, so I decided to get pregnant so they'd start treating me nice too.

"I loved being pregnant. It was really cool. All the men at work treated me like a queen and everyone was really nice. I never had so much attention. Complete strangers would come up to me on the street and ask me when I was due and want to touch my stomach. My friends at work threw me a baby shower and I got lots of neat gifts.

"The day Jamie was born was great. Lots of people came to the hospital to see the baby and see if I was all right. Even some of my family came and brought presents. It was the best day of my life. Jamie was perfect; she had all her little fingers and toes and I felt so proud.

"And it was great for the first few weeks after we left the hospital too. My cousin came over to help me out and friends dropped by. But then my cousin had to go home to take care of her own kids, and my friends got busy with their own lives, and I was left all alone with Jamie. It was like I suddenly wasn't important anymore. I remember crying myself to sleep every night for a week, realizing that my time in the spotlight was over and now all I had to look forward to was all this responsibility."

• **"Having a child will force me to grow up. It will make a woman (or a man) out of me."**

Even in this day and age, this is a common and pervasive reason many people have for wanting to become a parent. Many people are told this by their parents or grandparents so often that they come to believe it. Others, like my thirty-year-old client Maureen, believe having a baby will force them to become less selfish or more mature:

"I admit it, I'm selfish. I've only been focusing on myself and my own needs for a long time. But now I want to think about someone else instead of myself. I want to become a real woman. Having a baby is going to force me to grow up."

Merely becoming a mother does not make someone a *real* woman. Nor does having a baby make someone a man. As I told Maureen, if you feel having a baby will prove your womanhood or manhood to others or yourself, you need to rethink the situation. Becoming a parent requires maturity, responsible behavior, and integrity, the real definition of womanhood or manhood, and you need to possess these qualities *before* you decide to have a child.

While no one can argue that many people have become more mature and responsible with the birth of a child, it certainly does not guarantee it. You don't magically turn into a mature, caring person by the act of giving birth or fathering a child. It takes a lot of time and attention to acquire these qualities.

• **"I want a baby so I won't feel so all alone."**

This is a very common reason for wanting a baby, especially for single people, those whose parents have died, and those who aren't close to their parents or siblings. As my client Molly explained:

"My parents are deceased and I have no siblings. I'm thirty-five years old and I don't have a steady boyfriend. I'm tired of coming home to an empty house every night and spending every weekend alone. I want a child so I can have a family."

A child should never be seen as a pet or a companion to keep you company or fill an empty space in your life. When you have a child for any of these reasons you are creating a very unhealthy situation for both you and your child, one which encourages an unhealthy dependency between you and your child, and one which encourages your child to take care of your needs instead of the other way around.

• "I want to have children so they will take care of me when I'm old and sick."

No one relishes growing old alone. And we all can fall prey to the fear of becoming weak, vulnerable, and sick and having no one to care for us. But these fears do not present a good reason for having children.

This is what my client Joy shared with me:

"I've seen what my parents had to go through as they got old and sick. They were lucky to have me to take care of them. But who's going to take care of me? My dad is dead and my mother will undoubtedly go soon. I have no other family and at my age, my chances of marrying are slim. Why shouldn't I have a baby so someone will be there for me when I get old and sick?"

The reason this is not a good motivation for having children is that it is selfish.

To assume that by having a child you guarantee you'll be

taken care of is setting yourself up for grief and bitter disappointment and will inflict guilt and a tremendous burden on your adult offspring. Worrying about who will be there for you if you are childless is equally futile. Plan instead to provide for yourself now, both financially and emotionally, and make your decision about having a child one based on much thought and deliberation, not on fear of the future.

- **"I'm going to live forever through my children."**

Some people want to have a baby as a way of leaving a living testimony to their presence here, as a way of guaranteeing that their genetic line will continue. These people think of parenthood as "my link with the future," or "my immortality," as was the case with Mark:

"I want a child because I want to pass on the family name. I'm the only son and I feel it's my responsibility to make sure our name goes on."

When I asked Mark if he had any other reason for having a child, he said, "I'd have to say that's the primary reason, that and the fact that Cindy wants a baby. But I don't think I'll regret it."

Carrying on the family name, having someone to carry on the family business, or passing along a talent may seem to be noble and caring reasons to have children, but each is meant to meet the needs of the parents and not the child. In addition, these reasons may serve to create friction between a parent and a child and load the child down with guilt if they do not carry on the family name, tradition, talent, or family business.

A need for immortality ranks along with "Who will take care of me?" as a dubious motivation. As human as it is to want this, it should not be a primary reason for bringing a child into the world.

Some Positive Reasons for Wanting to Have a Child

Now let's discuss some positive reasons for wanting a child. You'll notice that the following list of positive reasons to have a child isn't half as long as the previous list. You'll also notice that the few positive reasons I do list are rather lengthy ones. This is because the most positive reasons for having a child are not short, quick, or easy. Many components have gone into making them optimum reasons.

- "I love my partner, we're in a healthy, committed relationship and a child seems to be a natural extension of our love and respect for one another. We've considered the issues carefully and discussed them openly and honestly and we're ready and able to devote our energy and resources to being loving, responsible parents."
- "I feel this is the right time for me to have a child. I have the time and energy to devote to a child and I am now mature enough, capable enough, and dedicated enough to be a good parent. I've read enough books about parenthood and observed enough children to feel that I know what I'm getting into."
- "I've always wanted children and my life would not be complete without them. I've worked on myself enough to know that I will be a good parent. I want the opportunity to share with my children the lessons I've learned, to pass on to them the love I was given."
- "I have so much love to give a child and I know I'll be a good parent. There are so many children out there who need parents. I'm not going into it blindly, I've done my research on the effects of neglect, abuse, and abandonment on a child and I know adopted children have unique problems. But I'm willing to deal with whatever comes up and to do whatever is necessary to provide my child the love and support he or she needs."

"I love kids. I love to watch them grow, to laugh at the silly things they do. I come from a large family and I'm surrounded by kids every day. They're one of the best joys in life as far as I'm concerned."

Becoming a parent involves so much dedication, sacrifice, and work that it is my belief that only those people who are sufficiently mature, adequately informed, and emotionally and financially capable should take on the task. Only those who are committed to being the best parents they can be, knowing at the same time that they will make mistakes, encounter problems, and suffer setbacks, disappointments, and heartaches along the way should take on the responsibility.

The information in the next chapter, along with the exercises and questions I present, will help you further discover whether your reasons are healthy ones. In addition, they will help you discover whether your reasons for wanting a child are firmly grounded in reality.

THREE

Avoiding Common Mistakes Potential Parents Make When Deciding

IT OFTEN HAPPENS that potential parents make their decision to have a child based on unrealistic expectations and fantasies, their own childhood experiences, on limited exposure to children, or on misinformation—plain and simple. Others allow themselves to be pressured into a decision by their mates, well-meaning family and friends, or by the media. In this chapter, we will discuss the most common mistakes people make when deciding whether to become parents and how you can avoid them.

Mistake #1: Basing Your Decision on Fantasy and Unrealistic Expectations

One of the most common mistakes potential parents make is to base their decision on fantasy and wishful thinking. In *The Motherhood Report*, which I referred to earlier, when women were asked why they decided to become parents, only about one in four women envisioned motherhood with any semblance of realism.

How about you? Do you think you're being realistic about what parenthood will be like? Before I give you a heavy dose of reality, complete the following exercise, allowing yourself to fantasize to your heart's content.

EXERCISE: What Is Your Fantasy?

1. As I'm sure you've already done, allow yourself to fantasize about what it would be like once you have your baby or adopt your child. What images come to mind?

2. Write down these fantasies for future reference, including such things as what you see yourself doing with your child, what emotions are stirred inside you, and how you will feel being a parent. As you write, think about:

a. How you imagine your life will change in a positive way if you were to become a parent
b. If you are in a relationship, the ways you foresee your relationship improving after becoming a parent
c. How you imagine your relationship with your parents will change for the better due to you becoming a parent
d. How you imagine your self-esteem and self-image will improve if you become a parent

The following are the most common types of fantasies and some of the unrealistic expectations potential parents have. You may be surprised to find that you have indulged in some of them.

Fantasies of Perfection

Unfortunately, what many people mean when they say, "I want a child" is "I want a perfect child." This was the case with the following people interviewed for the book.

- **Angela, age thirty-two, mother of two girls, ages four and six:**

"When I was contemplating having kids, I always imagined them as perfect little ladies and gentlemen—well-mannered, clean, sweet. I thought of how they'd look all dressed up, how I'd feel showing them off to other people. I was being so unrealistic! Sure, my kids look nice when they're dressed up, but that happens so rarely it's hardly worth mentioning. Mostly they're dirty from playing in the backyard or from having food smeared all over them. And the times they are at their worst is when company comes over. Then they always manage to make a mess or have a temper tantrum. My kids are far from perfect and it's been hard for me to adjust to this."

- **Anne, age thirty-five, and Randall, age thirty-seven, one child, age seven:**

"We had dreams of raising children who would be brilliant. I'd do all the right things, start teaching them early, send them to private schools, help them with their homework. And then we had Tommy, a child who doesn't even like school, who, no matter how much tutoring we arranged for, just doesn't get certain subjects like math and science, a kid who only wants to hang out with his friends and play sports. Not at all what we'd expected or hoped for."

- **Trisha, age thirty-nine, one child, age six:**

"When I decided to adopt a baby, it was because I felt I had things I wanted to pass on to a child, important things, like teaching a child to be tolerant and compassionate toward others, to have certain ideals and values. When the birth mother had a boy, I was elated because I felt I had a chance to raise a son the right way, to raise a boy who wouldn't be macho and chauvinistic like so many of the men I've had to deal with all my life.

"But Daniel is the most macho kid I've ever seen. All he ever talks about are guns and fighting. When he was four, he asked me if he could start karate classes like the boy next door and I agreed to it so he'd have a place to release all that energy. The other day he said to me, 'You know, Mom, boys are better than girls in everything.' I just stared at him. I couldn't believe he'd said that, after all I've tried to teach him."

Of course, most parents know that their children will not be perfect. After all, we've all seen two-year-olds having temper tantrums in the supermarket, and we all know about the problems with adolescents today. It is not that these parents were unaware of these realities. But in spite of this awareness, they clung to their fantasies of perfection, trying to convince themselves that their children would be the exceptions.

Those with perfection fantasies also try to convince themselves that they will be different from other parents, or more specifically, *better* than other parents, as was the case with Josh:

"I swore I was going to be a better parent than all those I was raised around. I'd always be cheerful and understanding, I'd always be available for my kids and I'd never get angry at them or yell at them. Unfortunately, it's easier said than done. I try but I find myself acting just like my parents did toward us kids, being irritable, yelling at them, telling them to get out of my hair. Hell, I even use the same expressions my father always used: 'Go play outside. Can't you get the hell out from under my feet for two seconds?' 'You good-for-nothing kids. Can't you do anything right?' "

This desire for perfection is, of course, completely understandable. Who doesn't want to be a perfect parent? Who doesn't want to recreate for their child the best moments of their childhood or relive their childhood in a more perfect way? But many parenting fantasies can leave a person unprepared for the day-to-day realities of having a child.

Confining Your Fantasies to Having a Child of a Particular Sex, Temperament, or Physical Appearance

Often, when potential parents fantasize about having a child, they picture a particular child, either a boy or a girl, and one with specific physical characteristics and/or temperament. This was the case with my client Holly:

"Every time I pictured the baby I would have, it was a little girl with curly blonde hair and beautiful big brown eyes, like all the women in my family. When the doctors told me I was going to have a boy, I couldn't believe how disappointed I was. I'd told myself I would be okay as long as I had a healthy baby. That it wouldn't matter to me what sex it was. But when it came right down to it, it did matter. I had to work hard to adjust to the fact I was having a boy. To top it all off, my son ended up being dark-haired like my husband's side of the family. I know I probably sound petty, but I guess I just wasn't being very realistic and it backfired on me. Of course, I love my son and he could have green hair for all I care now. It was just the initial shock, you know?"

Holly's experience is actually quite common. Most potential parents have preferences and most have fantasies that reflect those preferences. This is perfectly normal. But preferences aside, you must also be realistic. After all, you have little to no control over what sex your baby will be or what physical characteristics or temperament he or she will have. If you believe you will only be happy if your child is a particular sex, has specific physical characteristics, or has a specific temperament, you will need to adjust your fantasies to better reflect reality.

In addition, you also need to take into consideration the

possibility that your child could be born with a physical or mental handicap of some kind. While this is a very sobering thought, you need to be realistic—it could happen. If it did happen, how do you imagine you would handle it?

The following questions will help you consider all the possibilities and to think about your reactions to these possibilities.

Questions: Expectations and Reality

1. Do you prefer a boy or a girl child?
2. If you have a preference, what are your reasons?
3. What expectations do you have of a girl child? A boy child?
4. How do you imagine you will feel if the child is not the sex you prefer? Will you easily be able to accept a child who is not your preference?
5. What temperament do you imagine your child will have?
6. Do you have a preference for the type of temperament you'd like your child to have?
7. If you have a preference, what are your reasons?
8. Will you be able to accept a child who does not have such a temperament?
9. What do you imagine your child will look like?
10. Do you have a preference?
11. Will you be able to accept a child who does not have these physical characteristics?
12. What if your baby is born with a birth defect or other medical problem? Do you feel you would be able to handle it?

Not Thinking Beyond Having an Infant

Many parents, women in particular, tend to have unrealistic fantasies based on limiting their visions of parenthood to those of mothering an infant. Teresa is typical of many potential parents:

"When I was deciding whether or not to have a baby, all I thought about was how I would glow when I was pregnant, how I would feel knowing I'd actually created life from my own body, how it would feel to hold my baby in my arms. I loved the idea of having someone completely dependent on me. For some reason, I never got past these fantasies to think about what it would be like as my baby grew older. If I had, I realize now I may never have had a child."

Jennifer is also typical: "When I thought about having a baby, I only focused on how it would feel the moment I saw my baby for the first time, how much fun it would be to hold my baby in my arms and rock and sing her to sleep. Fortunately, my husband reminded me that the baby would eventually become a toddler, running around and getting into trouble every few minutes, requiring me to be constantly alert. I realized it wasn't going to be such a peaceful time after all."

It is important to envision your child not only as an infant but as a young child and eventually as a teenager. In this way, you can get a better idea about what parenting will actually be like. Since parenting is at least an eighteen-year commitment, you will need to be certain that you want not only a baby but also a toddler, not only a darling seven-year-old but a bratty thirteen-year-old as well. You will need to consider whether you are up for the task of not only taking care of the needs of a helpless, cuddly baby but those of a frightened six-year-old who is being bullied at school, a confused preteen who is beginning to develop sexually, and a rebellious sixteen-year-old who gets in trouble with the law.

Minimizing the Responsibility

Raised, as many of us were, as the "sitcom" generation, many people imagine that parenthood will be effortless and

joyous with problems that can be solved in half an hour.
Thinking of parenthood in this way is setting yourself up for
disappointment and frustration. In *The Motherhood Report*, the
more "benign" of potential parents' unrealistic fantasies are
called "fantasies of omission." These fantasies underestimate
the responsibilities and portray parenthood as simple and relatively effortless. The following statements, made by some of
those I interviewed, exemplify some of these types of fantasies:

- "I thought being a mother would be like playing house—you
  know, giving my baby a bath, dressing her in cute clothes,
  feeding her, holding and rocking her to sleep. I was so naive.
  I didn't realize I'd be doing these things several times a day
  and that a real baby doesn't just lie still while you do all these
  things. They cry and fuss and squirm, making everything
  twice as hard."
- "I thought the time after the baby was going to be like a
  vacation. I'd be off from work and have plenty of time to
  bond with my baby, just the two of us spending time together getting to know one another in a peaceful environment. But our time was far from peaceful. The first few
  weeks the house was constantly full of well-meaning relatives and friends and instead of helping, this just made things
  harder. I got almost no sleep at night and between diapering,
  feeding, laundry, and shopping, I had very little time to just
  quietly hold my new baby and when I did, I was so tired I
  almost fell asleep."
- "I'm a very well-organized person and I thought I would be
  able to manage a career and motherhood with no problems.
  But babies aren't on a schedule. They're totally unpredictable. Little did I know that a baby would totally disrupt my
  life to such an extent."
- "I thought mothering would come naturally to me. But I
  was totally unprepared for colic and diaper rash and figuring

out a way to pack up the baby and take him with me to the store."

Fantasies of Being a "Supermom" or "Superdad"

Still other fantasies revolve around your being a "supermom" or "superdad," capable of handling any and all responsibilities of parenthood, of being even-tempered and loving with your children at all times, and of managing a career and parenthood with few or no difficulties. The latter was my client Sara's fantasy:

"I thought it would be a snap. I have a lot of energy, so I figured all I needed was to get organized, read a few books, and arrange for good child care and there would be nothing to it. Brother, was I in for a shock!"

What Sara found out was that her baby was on his own timetable. He didn't go to sleep at night as she'd planned, so she often went into work exhausted. In addition, he was sick for the first six months of his life and she often had to take off work to provide for his medical care. On top of everything else, her nanny quit with no notice, so she had to take off still more time to interview new ones. What Sara discovered, as many new parents do, is that it is impossible to slot a baby into your life as if he were another item on a to-do list.

Moving from Fantasy to Reality

The unrealistic fantasies and expectations that many parents, and most women in particular, have of parenthood—whether they come from the media, from misperceptions of others' experiences, or from their own unmet needs—can be detrimental because they leave parents unprepared for the realities that face them.

The more realistic your fantasies and expectations are,

the easier time you will have coping with the more difficult aspects of parenthood. Those who have romanticized notions of parenthood, on the other hand, tend to have more negative feelings about parenthood once they became parents.

To further help you recognize whether your ideas about parenting are based on fantasy or reality, I suggest you spend lots of time around children. This will bring you face-to-face with many of the mundane aspects of child-rearing. Taking care of the children of friends and other family members for evenings, weekends, and vacations will give you an even more realistic picture of what it will be like to be a parent.

In addition, I suggest you engross yourself in parenting books and magazines, which will give you a good idea about the issues concerning parents today, issues that you yourself will have to deal with if you choose to become a parent.

Finally, talk to other parents about the rewards and trials of parenthood, with the understanding that their opinions will be strongly colored by their own experiences. Try to talk to a variety of mothers (young and older, married and single, struggling and financially set) in order to get a wider perspective.

Mistake #2: Buying into the Current "Baby Mania"

Another common mistake potential parents of both sexes make is buying into the current "baby mania." We are living in a time when the most popular kind of party is a baby shower; when high-profile couples as diverse as Tom Cruise and Nicole Kidman, James Carville and Mary Matalin, and even Pamela and Tommy Lee are spouting the glories of parenthood; and when television and magazine commercials abound with adorable babies and darling toddlers selling everything from bath soap to toilet paper. Is it any wonder that in this kind of baby-loving environment, more and more people are considering becoming parents?

While current generations of parents are no longer fed a constant diet of unrealistic portrayals of parenthood with television programs of the past, like *Leave It to Beaver*, the media still provides us with a great deal of romantic fantasies. A quick survey of the covers of parenting and other magazines will reveal a bounty of pictures of adorable infants and a multitude of blissful portraits of adoring mothers and babies. You see them everywhere—in print ads, on billboards, on television commercials—all those adorable babies, with their huge eyes and darling expressions.

LeeAnn, a woman I interviewed for the book, explained how she felt the media contributed to her decision to have a child:

"Everywhere I looked I saw darling little babies. In the supermarket, on the streets in their strollers. It seemed like everyone was suddenly having babies. And there were all those television commercials with those cute babies and toddlers. Who wouldn't want a baby when you see them everywhere like that? I knew I wasn't really mature enough to have a child, but it all got to me: all the baby pictures in magazines, all the baby movies, all the stars having babies. I thought I wouldn't be able to stand it if I didn't have one of my own."

If you feel you are being influenced by the media or by the fact that so many people are having children, try to remember that while babies can look cute and can really tug at your heartstrings, they aren't dolls to play with. They don't remain little babies forever and they are a huge responsibility.

Questions: Are You Being Overly Influenced by the Current "Baby Mania"?

1. Have you always wanted to have children?
2. If not, what made you change your mind?

3. When did you first begin to want them? What was going on in your life at the time?

4. Do you feel you've been influenced by the media to have a child? If so, how?

5. Do you think you've been influenced by the fact that so many of your friends are having children?

6. Do you think you've been influenced by the fact that so many celebrities are having children?

7. If you were not around so many babies, do you think you might feel differently about having one?

Mistake #3: Allowing Yourself to Be Pressured by Friends and Family

It is difficult not to give in when you are being pressured by your mate, family, or friends into having a child. When your mate continually lets you know how much he or she wants a child, when parents constantly pressure you for a grandchild, or when friends and family repeatedly ask you why you haven't started a family yet or warn you that if you wait too long you may not be able to conceive, the pressure can feel so overwhelming that it may sometimes feel easier to do as others wish than to keep fighting them.

But trying to placate others is not a good reason to have a baby. If you are hesitating about becoming a parent at this time or if you have real concerns about your ability to be a good parent, it is important to trust your instincts instead of giving in to the pressure.

In the *Motherhood* survey, those mothers who responded to outside pressure rather than having a baby out of a real desire tended to be less satisfied and less effective as mothers than other women. They became angrier at their children, had more negative feelings about their marriages, and their general feeling of well-being was lower than those who had more positive reasons for choosing parenthood.

Questions: How to Determine Whether You Really Want a Child or if You Are Being Pressured into It

1. What kinds of comments from your parents/spouse/ friends have felt like baby pressure?

2. What emotions do these comments evoke?

3. Do you sometimes consider going ahead and having a child now because your mate wants one so badly?

4. Why would you prefer to wait?

5. Do the comments of others about you remaining childless often affect you to the point that you begin to feel that maybe they are right after all? What do you think their motivation is when they make these remarks?

6. Do you have some real concerns about having children but feel you should have them anyway, just to please others or get them off your back?

Mistake #4: Buying into the Unrealistic Ways Other Parents Portrayed Their Experience

Another common mistake made when deciding whether or not to become a parent is buying into the unrealistic ways that other parents can sometimes portray parenthood.

Some people believe that mothers have a form of "amnesia" that causes them to forget how painful the experience of childbirth is. The reasoning is that this prevents them from being discouraged from having more babies. This same tendency toward "amnesia" may explain why some parents seem to "forget" the downside of parenthood when talking to a prospective parent, as was Jenny's experience:

"When I saw my friends' children, they were always on their best behavior and my friends seemed to only want to tell me about the positive side of parenting. When I asked them if they'd recommend it, they said, 'Of course. You'll love being a parent.' But for some reason, they neglected to tell me about

the downside. It seems like they had an investment in me becoming a parent like them, like women are programmed to
encourage other women to become parents. But just as soon
as I had my baby, the same women started complaining to me
about how hard being a parent is. Where were they before I
got pregnant?"

At other times, it seems that family and friends deliberately don't want to discourage prospective parents from having
children, as Marta experienced:

"My friends and relatives all told me how 'wonderful'
parenthood was. All they talked about was how cute their children were, the darling things they said and did. They didn't
bother to tell me about the pain and heartache—how scary it
is to be completely responsible for a baby and how frightening
it is when your child is sick. After I had my daughter and experienced all this firsthand, I asked them why they hadn't warned
me. They said they didn't want to discourage me with the
facts, that once you have a baby you're willing to put up with
all the pain, but that you might not be willing to have a baby
if you knew about it ahead of time."

Mistake #5: Basing Your Decision Solely on Your Own Childhood Experiences

Some potential parents make the mistake of thinking that
just because they had a happy childhood, relatively free of
problems, that their own child would have the same experience. Others expect that since their mothers seemed to be su-
perorganized, cheerful, and made parenting seem easy, that
they will experience it the same way, as was the case with
Tammy:

"My mother was a great parent. She managed to raise us
three kids, work out of the home, and still have time to be the
president of the PTA. I thought I'd be able to do it all too.
Unfortunately, I was wrong. I'm not my mother, I don't have
her skill for organizing and I don't have her energy."

Still others based their decision on the fact that they had been a "good" child and hadn't given their parents many problems and therefore, assumed their children would be the same. The following statement, made by my client Pamela, who was having a lot of problems with her son Adam, reflects this way of thinking:

"When I was a kid, I never gave my parents any trouble. I always minded because I wanted to please them. It's just so hard for me to understand why Adam refuses to mind. I guess I expected my kids to be like me and they just aren't."

While some potential parents have unrealistic fantasies of perfection and bliss, others envision parenthood in very negative terms, fraught with responsibility and drudgery and offering few rewards. Most of these people had very painful childhoods and therefore could not imagine parenthood as gratifying in any way. This is especially true for those whose parents constantly complained about how difficult being a parent was or who made them feel they were a burden on their parents, as was the case with Amanda:

"When my husband first started talking about having children, I told him he was dreaming—it just wasn't going to happen. My image of parenthood was so negative I just couldn't imagine ever wanting a child, much less more than one. My mother led me to believe that being a parent was the worst thing imaginable. She hated being a mother and I assumed I would too. She constantly told us kids how ungrateful we were and how she had to give up everything she'd ever wanted to do just to take care of us, so I couldn't imagine there was anything positive about being a parent."

Questions: Your Childhood Experiences

1. What messages about children and child-rearing did you get from your own childhood?

2. Do you remember any specific verbal messages that

you may have heard from your parents or other relatives regarding parenthood?

3. What kind of nonverbal messages did you receive about raising children and the parental role? For example, did your mother and father seem to enjoy being parents and enjoy their children or did they make it clear that they felt overwhelmed and put-upon?

4. How much do you feel your own childhood experiences are influencing your decision to become a parent? Make a list of the specific ideas you have about parenthood that you can trace to your own childhood experiences.

Mistake #6: Basing Your Decision on Limited Exposure to Children, Especially Limited Experience Being in the Caretaking Position

Think about it. How much do you really know about taking care of small children? How much hands-on experience have you had? If you are interested in exploring parenthood, real experience caring for children is an absolute must.

Even those with some caretaking experience come to realize its limitations, as Celia explained:

"I baby-sat all during high school and I guess I confused baby-sitting with parenting. In my naivete, I didn't realize that parenting is a lot harder, that you have to be with the kids all the time. In high school, I went home at the end of the evening. I didn't have to get up in the morning to the same kids, day after day."

Although many people (especially women) had extensive experience with children while baby-sitting in their teens, these experiences aren't necessarily a good predictor of how you will be with your own children. Often children are better behaved with caregivers than they are with their parents, with whom they feel more comfortable. Also, as a baby-sitter, you get a reprieve from the child when you return home. When you are a parent, there is no such reprieve.

You owe it to yourself, your partner if you have one, and especially to your future baby to make your decision based on reality, not fantasy, based on firsthand experience in the caretaking role, not the hype of the media or well-meaning friends and family. It is also important to recognize how your past and your hopes and dreams might be affecting how you envision a child. And last but certainly not least, your decision should be based on accurate information about what parenting entails: the trials and the tears as well as the happiness and joys.

FOUR

Dealing with Your Ambivalence

EVERY POTENTIAL PARENT experiences ambivalent feelings as they begin to consider having children. But these conflicting emotions can be very bewildering. By the time most people begin to think about children, they view themselves as fairly mature grown-ups—capable of knowing their own mind. The novelty of finding yourself so conflicted over a decision can be so confusing and overwhelming that you put all your efforts into trying to get past them instead of taking the time to look beneath for the emotions causing the turmoil.

The purpose of this chapter is to help you to look closely at some of the reasons *why* you might not want to have children and, having examined them, to come to some conclusions about them—to help you differentiate between those hesitations that serve as alarm bells and those that are naturally present at the start of any major undertaking.

As you answer the questions in the following pages, remember to try not to censor yourself. There are no right or wrong answers, rather, the intent is to encourage you to turn your thoughts inward and explore exactly what parenthood might mean to you and, equally important, what impact you as a parent might have on your child.

EXERCISE: Your Reasons for Not Wanting to Have a Child

In a previous chapter, you listed your reasons for wanting to have a child. This exercise will address your ambivalence about becoming a parent.

- List all the reasons why you do not want to have a child, all your fears and concerns about parenting. Once again, don't get bogged down in thinking too much. Try to write spontaneously without censoring yourself.

Getting to the Bottom of Your Ambivalence

People have various reasons for being uncertain whether they are ready to have a baby. There may be personal or career goals that they haven't met yet, they may not feel secure in their relationship (or may not have one), or they may not feel they are financially or emotionally secure enough.

For example, Connie and her husband Matt have been married for five years and they are both in their early thirties. All of Connie's friends already have children and she desperately wants a baby. She looks longingly in store windows at toys and baby clothes and listens with envy as her friends tell her one story after another about what cute thing their four-year-old did or how their seven-year-old is so smart in school.

Matt also wants children, but he feels they should wait. "There's so many things we haven't done yet," he insists. "We haven't bought a house yet, we haven't traveled. And I want to start my own business. I'm afraid that once we begin having babies, we'll never do any of these things."

Connie understands Matt's reluctance about getting tied down with kids because she has some of the same concerns. "I'm just starting to get somewhere at my company. By next year, I'll probably get promoted to an executive position and I know getting pregnant will jeopardize that. There's a part of me that says, 'Okay, let's wait a few more years.' But my desire to have a baby is sometimes overwhelming and it goes beyond all reason."

For many people, like Connie and Matt, ambivalence about having a baby revolves around the things they feel they will have to give up in order to become a parent. If this is true for you, the following exercise will help you clarify this issue.

EXERCISE: What Will I Give Up? What Will I Gain?

1. Make a list of all the things you imagine you will have to give up when you have a baby (i.e., freedom, peace and quiet, romance, time for your hobbies, a clean, lavishly decorated home).

2. Make a list of all the things you believe you will *gain* from having a baby (i.e., a family, the joy of watching a child grow up, the chance to give to your child what you didn't get).

If you are in a relationship, each of you should make separate lists. Do not share your lists until you have completed them. Then compare your lists with one another and use your lists as a starting point for a discussion.

The idea is not just to face the potential losses head-on but to also weigh them against the possible gains.

Many potential parents are torn between conflicting desires. The following are some common examples:

- "I think I'll miss something if I never have a child" *versus* "I don't think I'm willing to make the sacrifices necessary to have a child."
- "But wouldn't it be worth it for the pleasure of seeing a child grow and change?" *versus* "It looks to me like 90 percent pain for 10 percent pleasure. I don't think it's worth it."
- "I'm just being selfish" *versus* "I'm not being selfish, I'm just being realistic and looking out for what's best for me and the baby. My career doesn't leave much time for a child and I'm afraid my relationship couldn't withstand the added pressures of a child."
- "I'm too old to have a child" *versus* "People are having children at later and later ages all the time. I'm healthy and plan to live a long time, certainly long enough to raise a child."

This last example typifies the quandary many potential parents feel about the fact that they've waited so long to become parents:

- "I can't believe I'm actually turning forty and I still don't have a child. Most of my friends my age have eight- and nine-year-old kids."
- "I'm not sure I can even get pregnant. I've never been pregnant and as far as we know, my husband has never made anyone pregnant. You hear more and more about people who are having trouble, especially older couples, so I'm really worried."
- "So many of my friends waited until they were in their thirties to try to get pregnant. They'd been taking birth control pills for so long that a lot of them were taking six months to three years to get pregnant and some have had miscarriages and stillbirths. It makes me wonder whether it's because they waited too long. I feel like I'd better start trying now, whether I feel ready or not."

Some people are aware that they aren't necessarily *ready* to become parents, but because they are getting older, they feel they *should* become parents.

- "I want to be a young parent. My mother was forty when she had me and my dad was almost fifty and they didn't have the energy to play with me. I want to enjoy being a parent, not have it be a drudge, and I notice I'm getting more and more tired all the time."
- "I want to have kids while I'm young, so my husband and I will still be young enough to enjoy an early retirement. I don't want to be going through all the hassles of dealing with teenagers while I'm in my fifties, like some parents I've known."

There are many other reasons why you may experience confusion and ambivalence about becoming a parent. Many of those who are conflicted feel that they are ill-equipped to assume the responsibilities of parenthood. This is what my client Nina told me:

"I want a baby, but I really don't think I'd make a very good mother. It's an awful lot of responsibility and frankly, that scares me. I'm not sure I'd do the right things. And I'm a pretty selfish person. I don't know that I want to devote the next eighteen years to raising a child."

It is important to note that studies such as *The Motherhood Report* found that women with these kinds of concerns and fears who went on to become mothers tended to be less-satisfied and less-effective mothers than other women. While it is difficult to say whether this was because their fears became self-fulfilling prophecies or whether they reflected a realistic evaluation of themselves, these women tended to become angrier at their children more often, had more negative feelings about their marriages, and had a generally lower feeling of well-being than the majority of mothers surveyed.

Another major contributing factor to many potential parents' ambivalence is that many women and men alike feel uncertain, squeamish, or even fearful about pregnancy and this affects their desire to have a child. This was the case with Lillian:

"The major conflict I have about becoming pregnant is my fear of hospitals and surgery. I know most women get through it just fine, but every time I hear about a woman having a cesarean section, it makes me cringe. My doctors tell me that cesareans are perfectly safe and that many women have them successfully, but that isn't reassuring at all. I mean, they cut open your stomach, for God's sake."

In addition, many women, in particular, are anxious about the physical changes that result from pregnancy and birth, as it was with Rene:

"I want a baby very badly, but I just hate the fact that most women gain so much weight after they have a child. I know a few who didn't, but it was because they worked out every day before they had their baby and started working out again right away after they delivered. I'm just not sure I would have the willpower to do that, especially while I'm pregnant. And it's not just the weight, it's the spread. Even the women who haven't gained weight get wider in the hips and behinds. Let's face it. No matter what you do to prevent it, having a baby changes a woman's body for good."

It is understandable for women (and their partners) to be concerned about the inevitable changes that occur to a woman's body as a result of pregnancy and childbirth. When a woman becomes pregnant, her body alters before her eyes.

If you have these or other concerns, the following exercise will help you and your partner gain insight into them.

EXERCISE: **Picturing Yourself**

For Women

   1. Close your eyes and picture yourself:
   • during early pregnancy when you just begin to show
   • during late pregnancy when you are quite large and un-
     comfortable
   • during childbirth
   • while nursing

   2. Do these physical changes attract or repel you? Pay
particular attention to the feelings surrounding the ones that
repel you. What are these emotions? Fear? Shame or embar-
rassment? Following are some common reactions:
   • Does fear of childbirth pain affect your desire to get
     pregnant?
   • Are you held back by thoughts of getting fat and staying
     fat?
   • How do you imagine your body will change after giving
     birth?
   • How do you imagine you will feel about your new
     body?

   If you have a partner, discuss your thoughts with him or
her.

For Men

   1. Close your eyes and picture your partner:
   • during early pregnancy when she just begins to show
   • during late pregnancy when she is quite large
   • during childbirth
   • while nursing

   2. How do you think you will react to these changes?
Will you find her more attractive, less attractive, or the same?
   Share your feelings and concerns with your partner, being

as honest as you possibly can. It is far more important to share them with your partner now than to let them affect your decision to have a baby or to allow them to negatively affect your relationship during pregnancy and after childbirth.

Female Ambivalence

Women are ambivalent about becoming mothers for many reasons, some of which we've already touched on. In addition to the above concerns, women are ambivalent due to the tremendous responsibility involved in child-rearing. Even today, in our more liberated environment, most women, even those who are in a relationship, generally end up being the primary caretaker. Because of this, they tend to feel the full weight of responsibility will fall on their shoulders. Naturally, this causes them to be more cautious about becoming a parent, in spite of the fact that most women have strong desires in that direction.

Another reason for women's ambivalence is the strong connection between mothers and daughters. The relationship between mother and daughter, even when it's a healthy one, is fraught with conflicts concerning the need to move away and the need to stay connected, to emulate and to differentiate. No matter how successful a woman is in separating from her mother and how genuinely different her life is from the one her mother had, a woman can still worry that she will automatically and magically be transformed into her mother as soon as she gives birth. This is because to have a child is to participate directly and concretely in another mother/child relationship, pulling a woman back into her own past, evoking feelings and experiences she has put behind her. She fears either that she could turn into her mother or that a baby will emulate aspects of her mother that upset her—be depriving, controlling, or intrusive.

When a woman chooses to be childless, she severs a major, literal tie with her mother and powerfully differentiates herself from her mother's life. Even those women who love their mother dearly may choose to remain childless as a way of not copying their mother in this important way. This, from a daughter's perspective, is perhaps the most fundamental way to do so.

Still another reason for women's ambivalence is their concern that their partner will not be a good parent. Women tend to be more concerned than men about their partner's parenting ability, and this may cause them to hesitate no matter how much they want a child. Some see qualities in their partner that concern them, such as irresponsibility, difficulties dealing with emotional burdens or emotional volatility, while others have concerns about the way their partner was raised. My client Summer had both concerns:

"I want a baby so badly, but I'm worried that Ray won't be a very good father. His own father was very cruel to him and Ray tends to have a sharp tongue himself. He seems to like kids and likes to play with them, but he tends to play rough and he often acts like a kid himself, wanting his own way, that kind of thing. He's a very poor sport and he always gets mad when he loses. I've talked to him about it, but he gets so defensive. I'm afraid of the kind of example he'd be to our kids."

Interestingly, as you'll see in the section on male fears, many men are aware of the legacy of abuse or cruelty in their families and have similar concerns. An open discussion with your partner can do a lot to focus your concerns and help you make plans for how to address them.

Female Fears Concerning Parenthood

In addition to their ambivalence and their concerns, many women have fears that prevent them from becoming parents. Some of the most common follow:

1. Fear of no longer being physically attractive to their partner during their pregnancy or when they find themselves in the role of a "mother."

This is a common fear, most often brought on by listening to horror stories of husbands who strayed during their wives' pregnancy. But many men find pregnant women extremely attractive and it is important for women who are considering having a baby to not place too much importance on their physical appearance and to realize that their partner loves them for other reasons than how they look. If a woman is really concerned that her husband will fall out of love with her or become unfaithful due to her pregnancy, it is important that she address these issues with her husband before deciding.

Some men do have a difficult time perceiving their wife as both a sexual being and a nurturing mother and so this fear is well founded. Some just need time to make the transition, while others need overt approaches from their wives, showing they are still sexually interested.

2. Fear of being unable to lose the weight they've gained during pregnancy

Women receive contradictory messages about their roles as women. On the one hand, we are supposed to bear and nurture children; on the other, we're also supposed to be thin, glamorous, and perpetually youthful with smooth, flawless skin.

Some women have a more difficult time losing weight after pregnancy than others. This is due to several factors, including genetics, how active a woman was able to be during and shortly after pregnancy and whether there were any complications in either the pregnancy or the birth.

Instead of buying into the media hype of the perfect body, it is important for women to come to terms with their body and see it as part of a continuum—an ever-changing, miraculous machine.

3. Fear of losing themselves or losing momentum in their career

Many women fear that having a child will rob them of their hard-won independence or interfere with their career plans, as was the case with Hayley:

"My mother gave up her career in order to raise us kids. She ended up being a bitter, angry woman who resented us kids and my father. I don't want to end up like that. I've worked hard to achieve the things I've accomplished and I'm not sure I want to jeopardize it all to raise children. Sure, I know women today are supposed to be able to do it all, but I haven't known any who've actually accomplished it, who haven't had to sacrifice something."

Male Ambivalence

Today, we see a very different picture of how fathers are supposed to act regarding parenthood. Movies like *Three Men and a Baby* and books such as *FatherLove: What We Need, What We Seek, What We Must Create* by Richard Louv, *The Father's Almanac* by S. Adams Sullivan, *Questions from Dad* by Dwight Tilley, and *Pregnant Fathers: Entering Parenthood Together* by Jack Helnowitz, as well as *Her Father* by Bill Henderson, point to the growing role dads are playing in the family. But no matter how much things seem to have changed, the truth is, some men have confused and conflicting attitudes about children. Many of them appear to be apprehensive about fatherhood. They often need coaxing—and sometimes outright coercion—in order to "get into the baby thing." Many men don't relate well to infants, preferring young children who can walk and talk—who "have some personality," as many new dads put it.

And often men are not interested in having children at all. Those men who aren't interested in fatherhood are reluctant to confess it in this "baby-loving" culture. They are often branded immature or irresponsible since fatherhood is seen as a rite of passage in this culture and a sign of maturity and willingness to take on responsibility. For instance, for years in the business world, there was an unspoken belief that a "family man" was more reliable and more promotable.

As we all know, most men need to learn from females how to be more sensitive and open to their feelings. But it is my belief that women need to learn to be more realistic from men, especially when it comes to the parenthood decision. The truth is, men tend to be more honest about the realities of parenting than women.

Men can afford to be more realistic and less idealistic about parenthood because they have less of their self-esteem invested in it than do women. Their role in life is not defined by parenthood, whereas many women have been encouraged, coached, and expected to be mothers since they could walk. Because men can afford to be more realistic, and therefore more dispassionate toward parenthood, they tend to notice the hassles as well as the joys and rewards.

And even though men tend to be more sensitive than women on the subject of selfishness (because the charge of selfishness seems to be leveled at them more often), they are more comfortable with the concept of selfishness, less daunted by it than are women, as you can see from what my friend Seth had to say:

"Having children is an unbelievable sacrifice and frankly, I'm not sure I'm willing to make it. I love our life just as it is. Why would I want to give up the socializing, the travel, the fun that my wife and I now share to stay home and baby-sit kids? I know that makes me sound like I'm selfish, but I'm just being honest about how I really feel."

Men can also tend to be more realistic about how children

will affect their relationship with their wife and their sex life in particular. This is what my client Don told me:

"My wife and I have a fabulous sex life and I don't want to do anything to mess it up. We've all heard how children affect a couple's sex life and I'm afraid it will ruin ours. My wife assures me it won't happen to us, but I've heard other couples say the same thing and found out later that having kids did affect their sex life. Sex is more important to me than it is to my wife. I know she could adjust to it. I'm just not sure I could."

Men are also more likely to view the parenthood issue as a quantitative, measurable commodity and to ask themselves such questions as: "How will it affect my life?" "Do I have the financial resources?" "What will this do to my life plans?" "How will it change our lifestyle?" After asking himself these questions, Barry came to the following conclusion:

"The fact is, we just can't afford a child now. It's that simple. My wife says we will manage, that it's far more important for a child to have loving parents than it is for them to have money, but I don't agree. I came from a poor family and I saw what it did to my mother and father to have to watch us go off to school in hand-me-downs. I don't want that to happen to my kids."

Men also tend to be more realistic about their own limits and liabilities, as was the case with Phillip:

"I'm a very quiet, introspective person. I don't like being around a lot of people and when I'm around children I tend to get very uncomfortable. I'm also very sensitive to loud noises and when I'm around children I get very irritated. I believe very strongly that I shouldn't have kids for all these reasons, but my wife says I'll feel different when it's my own kids. I don't think so."

Male Fears Concerning Parenthood

Men also have specific fears that can prevent them from wanting to become fathers, such as the following:

1. Loss of control

The issue of control is an important one to men in all aspects of their lives and many indicate that it is of particular concern in child-rearing.

Parenthood is one area of a man's life where he feels out of control and sometimes out of the loop altogether. The formidable control that a mother exerts over every facet of her child's life can be very intimidating.

In addition, many men see a child as an interloper in their relationship with their wife or lover and fear the loss of intimacy and the attention they will receive from their mates.

And in a society where half our marriages end, many men fear having children only to lose them if a divorce occurs. While women may end up with less financial security when a divorce occurs, men suffer from a loss of intimacy and connection in their personal relationships with their children. Since a standard custody agreement has Dad seeing the kids every other weekend and perhaps a Wednesday in between, men have reason to be fearful about the potential pain and loss.

In addition, many men have been stripped of their custody rights yet made to pay child support while having no input in their children's lives. Hearing about such negative experiences from other men can certainly frighten and intimidate those men who are undecided about parenthood.

2. Concerns about their personal history

Interestingly, it is often men, more than women, who worry about passing on abusive or dysfunctional behavior from childhood. They realize that one of the key factors in becoming an abusive parent is having learned it from an abu-

sive parent and they are concerned about passing on negative behavior to their children.

Not all men react to their past in this manner. Many men who were abused as children believe that if they work hard they can overcome the abuse of their own childhoods. But these men generally have a strong sense of who they are and where they have come from and these facts play more than a small part in their decision about parenting. They do not try to fool themselves into believing that it won't happen with them. They know that it will require an enormous amount of work for them to do better.

3. Concern about the impact on one's current lifestyle and ability to provide for a family

Men have a tendency to think longer and harder about the specific effect a child will have on their lifestyle. Unless they are particularly motivated to have a child and see specific advantages, many men opt out of parenthood for this reason.

Rob and Linda were considering becoming parents but they both had some reservations about it, mostly on Rob's part. They decided to come in for counseling in order to work out some of their issues.

It turned out that Rob was a very logical man. So much so that he insisted that he and his wife lay out the positive and negatives of raising a child on paper. Linda resisted at first. "Why are you being so logical about this? What about feelings? Don't you care that I want a baby so much? Don't you want to experience being a father?"

Rob stuck to his guns and even wrote out a list of things for Linda to consider. He seemed to think of everything, from the needs of a baby to the needs of a college-age child. When I commended him on doing this, he said, "It's just that I need to know what's going to happen to our lives. And I need to know if we can afford a child, emotionally as well as financially; if our marriage can withstand the pressure."

functions, self-esteem, ability to express emotions, intelligence, and tendencies toward one or another sexual orientation and found that lesbian and gay families can and do offer what children need to grow into healthy, happy, and well-adjusted children.

Those who are most ambivalent are those who found growing up as lesbians or gay men to be painful, frightening, shameful, and isolating and those who endured teasing or rejection from others because they were different. They imagine their own children will have to go through similar experiences of social ostracism and will grow up feeling bad about themselves. They wonder whether it is fair to thrust their own children into such a difficult life and worry that their children will eventually become angry and resentful at them for doing so. This was the situation with Jesse:

"I know how cruel kids can be and I just don't know if I want to subject a child to that kind of teasing. I didn't have a choice about being gay, but I do have a choice about whether or not to bring a child into this world who will have to suffer like I did. I just wish I didn't want a child so much."

While Jesse and other gays have valid concerns considering our current social climate, the fact is that these fears are not becoming a reality. To the contrary, most gay and lesbian families instill a great deal of pride in their children and provide them with the tools to deal with prejudice. As in other families that contain oppressed minorities, children of gays and lesbians have to understand and deal with the problems of ignorance and bias. Depending on the social climate of their environment, these children often make selective decisions about whom to tell and, in general, only rarely encounter any significant homophobic treatment. In instances where this occurs, these children are often more prepared to handle it, than children in more traditional families.

Tim, a fifteen-year-old, summed it up for me as follows:

"Growing up with lesbian parents taught me a lot about prejudice. People who are prejudiced are just threatened by the differences between people. Both my moms taught me that being different just means that you're different, not that you're better or worse. I think I learned more about tolerance and being nonjudgmental than most kids I know and I owe it all to the way I was brought up."

The fact is that children will be hurt by teasing, shaming, and social ostracism whether their parents are gay or straight. All you can do as a responsible parent is to prepare them and teach them how to handle it.

There is a downside to lesbians and gays having children. Their children often get tired of having to explain their families to schoolmates. This starts from the time they are asked to draw pictures of their family and continues on through Parents' Day and other special occasions when their parents show up together. Some children have admitted to feeling embarrassed by the situation, even though they weren't necessarily teased by other children. But being embarrassed and having negative feelings about parents is not particular to children of gays and lesbians and is not the same as being psychologically damaged by the situation.

Also, children of lesbians often go through some sad feelings about not having a father, just as children of gay men often miss having a mother. But every child, whatever kind of family he or she comes from, sometimes wishes their family was different. If you are willing to listen to your child's feelings with compassion and respond without defensiveness or imposing guilt, your child will eventually come to terms with these disappointments in life.

Most gay and lesbian parents recognize the importance of their children having relationships with both men and women, but those relationships do not have to be with parents. Just as single parents of both sexes make a point of bringing people of the opposite sex into their children's lives, you can too. My client Michael explained to me how he and his partner Eric plan to deal with the fact that their child will be raised by two fathers and no mother:

"I came from a very large Italian family: four brothers and two sisters. Our house was filled with the sounds of children laughing and squealing. Most of my brothers and sisters have children and I'm very close to all my nieces and nephews. Almost every weekend, I take a bunch of them to the show or to the park.

"My family knows I'm gay and they've all grown to accept it. Sure, it was difficult when I first came out to them, but we're such a close family that they all eventually came around once they became more educated and realized that I'm happy being gay. I've talked to them about how they'd feel if Eric and I had a child and they're mostly supportive. We have a close female friend who has agreed to have our child and even though she travels a great deal, she wants to have a role in our baby's life. Eric and I feel that will be important for our child, especially if we end up adopting a girl. But mostly, we're not worried. That baby is going to have three parents, four grandparents, six aunts and uncles, and seventeen cousins. That baby is going to be loved!"

Whether your child will suffer from the discomforts of prejudice that you may have felt has something to do with how open you are able to be about your family structure in your neighborhood, in your family, and in the community at large. The degree of openness you are able to feel and maintain, as well as the amount of community support you have about your openness, will have a tremendous influence on how comfortable your children will be with their friends and schoolmates.

In general, I recommend you follow the same guidelines I set out for all potential parents in making your decision about becoming a parent.

It is important to view your feelings of ambivalence in a positive light. They are either indications that you need to resolve some issues before making your final decision or they are warnings that parenthood may not be for you. Continue to be honest about your reservations and concerns and give yourself time to resolve them before even attempting to make such an important decision. The following chapters will address many of your concerns.

At this point, some of you may now be certain you want a child but aren't sure you are ready to have one at the present time. In Part II, I will not only help you determine your readiness but suggest ways to become better prepared.

FIVE

Deciding Whether You Want to Be a Single Parent

WE ARE rapidly headed away from the conventional two-parent model of family, with only 11 percent of U.S. families consisting of both biological parents living in the same house with their children. Over half of all children born today will, for one reason or another, live in a single-parent family at some point in their lives. In addition, for some, the single-parent family is an outright choice.

More and more single people are contemplating having a child but aren't certain they can handle the responsibility on their own. They are torn between their desire to have a baby and their belief that it would not be fair to raise a child as a single parent.

In this chapter, I will help those of you who are single women and men contemplating having a child. I will present the pros and cons of single parenthood, as well as the issues you need to consider before making your final decision.

The Positives and Negatives of Single Parenting

While most people will agree that a child raised in a household with both a mother and a father has certain advantages over a child raised in a one-parent household, we need to keep in mind the fact that the so-called "alternative family" (single-parent family, stepparent family, families with gay or lesbian parents) is now more common than the traditional family. And while many people believe that having a child in a family with two loving parents is still the ideal situation, after many years of overidealizing the traditional family, we now know that it was not perfect. The truth is that children can be raised successfully in other kinds of families as well.

More and more, experts are discovering that what is most important is that a child feels secure, loved, and wanted and that there be minimal family disruption—not whether he or she is raised by one parent or two. Most experts in child development now say (albeit cautiously) that while it is too soon to be sure, it appears that the children of single parents have as good a chance of turning out well as any other child.

In addition, since children born to single parents have *not* experienced the loss of a parent or the breakup and disruption of a family the way over half the children of married parents have, they have some advantages over these children.

A study entitled "Family Structure and Adolescent Behavior" by Demo and Acock at the University of Missouri Department of Human Development and Family Studies brings still further good news for single parents. The authors found that adolescents whose mothers never married have fewer conflicts with their parents, better school grades, and fewer personal and adjustment problems than children from either divorced or stepparent families.

Part of the reason for this may be that children raised by a single parent by choice know they are wanted and they sense their importance in their parent's life. In addition, they tend to get a great deal of attention. Since a single parent doesn't have to cope with the needs of a spouse who also requires their time and attention, they can devote a great deal of their energy to their child.

However, on the downside, a family of two tends to have a more intense relationship with one another than those found in a larger family, and this greater intensity necessitates that single parents be especially clear and consistent about their approach to discipline and in setting limits with their children.

It is not healthy for a child to be raised with one parent as his or her only source of nurturing. Nor is it healthy for a parent to look to his or her child as the only source of connectedness. You will need to make sure that both you and your child do not become too isolated from others, that you both have outside interests and relationships, and, most important, that you allow others to love and care for your child.

Arranging for this will also combat another major drawback of being a single parent—the fact that all the responsibility of raising your child will fall on your shoulders. Whereas couples can share tasks and responsibilities, parenthood is a full-time job for single parents, who have to be both mother and father to their children. Couples can also provide a balance in terms of who is the disciplinarian and who is the nurturer. You, on the other hand, will need a strong support system for both emotional and physical backup.

Are You a Good Candidate for Single Parenting?

Since this style of parenting is not for everyone, it is important that you ask yourself whether you are a good candidate for single parenting. Some people have an easier time dealing with the stresses of single parenthood than others. For example, if you are a flexible person who easily accepts differences among people, you are more likely to feel comfortable with a family structure that is atypical. In order to help your future child feel good about being part of an alternative family, you will have to be able to present the concept of being different in a positive light. On the other hand, if you tend to be conservative or have very definite ideas about right and wrong, you might find that you are not as comfortable with choosing an unconventional path.

Also, since our society is still not completely supportive of single mothers (and certainly not of single fathers), it will help if you are the kind of person who doesn't look to others for approval and who can maintain your equilibrium and your self-esteem without a great deal of external support. For example, your family and friends may not be supportive of your decision and many single parents by choice are accused of being selfish for wanting to be a single parent or for depriving their baby of a father or mother. In order to counter these feelings and comments, you will need to be positive about your decision and be able and willing to stand by it. If you have the courage of your convictions and the support of a few significant people, the opinion of the mass majority of people shouldn't be as important to you.

Since a good support system is crucial to a single parent, particularly in the earliest stages of parenthood, it will help tremendously if you are the kind of person who has a support system already in place and/or can comfortably reach out to others for help.

Another issue to consider is whether you have adequate financial resources to support both yourself and a child. You can raise a child alone without being wealthy, but you need to be prepared for the necessary expenses, such as food, housing, health care, day care, clothes, school expenses, and recreational supplies and activities. You will need to put money aside for emergencies, vacations, and ultimately, for college.

Still another consideration is whether you will be able to spend an adequate amount of time with your child. As your child's only parent, you won't have the luxury of having a partner to share the responsibilities of child-rearing and you alone will have the responsibility to provide your child quality time with a parent. It certainly would not be fair to the child if you are rarely home during the child's waking hours.

And finally, it is important that you are the kind of person who can handle stress well, since you undoubtedly will be under a great deal of stress, particularly during the first year or two of parenthood. It is especially important that you have found constructive outlets for stress and frustration, as opposed to losing your temper or taking out your frustration on others.

Questioning Your Motives

Another question to ask yourself when deciding is: "Why am I considering single parenthood at this time?" In Chapter Two, we focused on your motives for wanting a child, but the desire to be a single parent requires even closer scrutiny.

EXERCISE: Why Do You Want to Be a Single Parent?

- Write down all your reasons for wanting to become a single parent at this time (i.e., time is running out and you don't want to wait any longer for an appropriate partner; you don't think you want to get married, but you do want a child).
- Read your list over carefully and pay attention to how you feel about each response. Do you feel satisfied with your answers or do they present some concerns?

Now answer the following questions as honestly as possible and be as open as you can be to the comments that follow each question.

1. Are you contemplating having a baby because you are often lonely and think having a child would help give you comfort and companionship?

It would be unfair of you to expect a baby to provide your life meaning or provide you company or nurturing. Hopefully, your life is already rich and satisfying and your desire to have a baby is coming more out of a wish to share your happiness with a child than to have a child create happiness for you. Also, in order to be a good single parent, you need to be able to nurture yourself when needed and not place those needs onto your child.

2. Do you think that having a baby will preserve the bond between you and the man (or woman) you love, even if the relationship were to end?

If this is the case, you need to think again. Having a child is not a guarantee that the relationship will continue and this is not a good reason to have a baby. A child should never be used as a ploy or manipulation and you may take your anger out on the child should the man reject you or the child.

3. Are you trying to shock or hurt someone or to prove that you can do something on your own?

Some women decide to maintain a pregnancy or keep a baby in reaction to their parents' or others' negative reactions or insistence that they either terminate the pregnancy or give the baby up for adoption. Others do so in order to prove they can do something on their own. Once again, these are not positive reasons for having a child and will undoubtedly backfire on you later.

4. Do you have unresolved issues about the opposite sex and relationships, and are you sure that you are not angry at men (or women) or trying in some way to get even with a particular man (or woman)?

It's important to place a high value on male and female relationships in order to give your child a realistic perspective of the world. No matter what the sex of your child, it is most important not to have negative feelings toward the opposite sex.

Single Mothers

If you are considering becoming a single mother, you are not alone. Thirty percent of all American children are now born to unmarried mothers. This includes lesbian women in partnerships who have decided on self-insemination. The numbers of Mothers Outside of Marriage, or MOMs (a term coined by Andrea Engber and Leah Klungness, Ph.D., in their book *The Complete Single Mother*) or Single Mothers by Choice, or SMCs, has been growing at a rate of more than 60 percent in the last decade. Nearly a quarter of America's never-married women are now mothers.

The highest rates of increase are among white women over the age of twenty. The increase was particularly sharp among educated and professional women. Among white women and women who attended college, the percentage more than doubled; and for women with professional or managerial jobs, it nearly tripled.

Contrary to popular stereotypes about unmarried mothers, statistics show that single mothers are usually working women who have decided that having a child is more important than any disapproval they may face. Although these women may believe that a nurturing mother and father is the ideal family for a child, they are realistic about accepting the fact that Mr. Right might not materialize.

The MOM label encompasses those who arrived at motherhood by accident, those who consciously chose to become pregnant, and those who became adoptive mothers. Technically, there is a difference between a Single Mother by Choice (SMC) and a MOM. For example, when the television sitcom character Murphy Brown had her baby, she was referred to as an SMC who was mocking fatherhood. But Murphy was really a MOM. Unlike a true SMC, who chose motherhood through adoption, donor insemination, or intercourse, Murphy's pregnancy was an accident. But whether they chose donor insemination or chose to raise their babies on their own after realizing they were not in a partnership with someone who wanted to be a father or who are not father material, all single mothers have many of the same experiences, beginning with the reasons why they chose to be single mothers:

- Their mate didn't share their feelings.

    Often women find themselves in a relationship with a man who doesn't want children. This may be because the man never made this clear or because the woman felt he would change his mind if she became pregnant.
- Their mate can't make up his mind.

    Some women decide to have a child on their own because they don't want to continue waiting around for their mate to decide to become a father.
- Mr. Right hasn't shown up.

    Many women have grown tired of waiting for Mr. Right or even Mr. Adequate to show up or may fear that by the time he appears they will be too old to safely bear children. Some go the sperm bank route, while others become pregnant by someone they have cared for or with whom they have been involved.
- Their internal clock is ticking fast.

    Many women begin to become anxious about their biological clocks at around age thirty.

- Their partner left them.

     Some women who planned their pregnancy with their mate end up being single mothers when their mate leaves the relationship. There may have been difficulties all along and they may have felt that a child could bring them closer together or the strain of impending parenthood may have caused them to split apart.

- Their partner had problems they didn't want to impose on their child.

     Some women decide that they do not want their new child exposed to certain behavior on the part of their partner, behavior such as excessive drinking or verbal or physical abuse. Women who have put up with such behavior for a long time often decide that they are not going to expose their child to it.

- Their birth control didn't work.

     Many women find that once they discover they are pregnant, even if it was an accident, they are thrilled at the idea of being a mother. Others, especially women who have had previous abortions, feel "this pregnancy is meant to be."

Common Concerns and Potential Problems

     As a single mother, you will have special concerns and experience unique problems. Some of these concerns and problems are:

     1. The main problem for many mothers alone is not the absence of a man but the shortage of money, as women still continue to earn less in our society.

     Unless you are independently wealthy, have a family who agrees to support you and your child, or have a lucrative career, you will undoubtedly experience stress about money issues during your child's entire life. Since you will be the sole source of income and support for your child you will need to continually put money aside for emergencies such as your own or your child's illnesses, accidents, or the possibility that you may at some time be unemployed.

2. It is important that single expectant mothers be prepared for the physical and emotional changes they will go through, before, during, and after childbirth.

You need to keep in mind that you won't have a partner to share feelings with you or comfort you during the hormonal shifts and mood swings that go along with pregnancy. Also, you should arrange to have a friend or family member be your labor coach and help you out the first few weeks after birth.

A parent alone—and any woman who does not have emotional support and practical help from her partner—needs a good support network. It is especially important to have a close friend or group of women with whom you can talk freely about your pregnancy, your birth experience and the stresses and joys of motherhood. This will help put the stresses of motherhood in perspective and will be a significant factor in helping to prevent depression.

3. Another important necessity for a single mother is to line up good child care.

This is especially true if you plan on working outside the house, but even those who work in the home need to get out and do something quite different from mothering from time to time to avoid feeling isolated, overly stressed, or depressed.

4. Another area for concern is the fact that there is no second parent to help the child emotionally separate from the intense early tie to the mother, nor is there a built-in male figure to provide a role model for your child.

In the traditional family, the father has always been acknowledged for playing two vital roles in the lives of his children. First, he helps his offspring develop a sense of their own competence and independence outside the powerful intimacy of the mother/child relationship and to emotionally separate from the mother. He provides an alternative to the mother's point of view, style, and temperament.

The father is usually the most "significant other" in the baby's life and, as such, helps the baby learn about comings and goings, transitions, separations, and nonmother nurturing. The child learns, through the father's in-and-out schedule, how to develop a mental image of something longed for and trusted, though not always actually present.

Because the child is accustomed to separations from the father, he or she often turns to him for help in differentiating itself from its mother. When the "terrible twos" arrive, a time when the child actively begins separating from mother, the father is pursued by the child as the parent who is already seen as separate, novel, interesting, and a source of adventure.

However, this function does not necessarily have to be performed by the child's biological father. If you understand and accept that your child will sometimes need a third person to step in and take over, you can encourage a friend or member of your family to serve this function.

Second, the father contributes in a powerful way to the sexual identity formation of his children. It is very valuable for both girls and boys to have a man involved with them in some intimate way from their earliest years. Part of the reason is that it is important that your child feels comfortable and gets along with both sexes. But even more important is the fact that boy children need a relationship with a man in order to have a role model for masculine identification, and a girl needs it for the experience of loving and being loved by a man. This is so important that it would behoove you to find such a man to play this role in your child's life. The man does not have to be the child's father, but he can be any loving, reliable man who is or would like to be part of your life.

5. You need to be sure you are comfortable being the sole disciplinarian for your child.

Since the emotional bond between a mother and her child can become overly intense when there isn't a second parent, it is especially important that you feel comfortable setting and maintaining clear limits with your child. Single moms need to be able to hold their children accountable for their actions and feelings. It's particularly important for mothers of sons to have expectations about how their sons should behave—and not to let them off the hook because they are afraid of saying or doing the wrong things or to dismiss unacceptable behavior with "Oh, it's just a boy thing."

If You Have a Relationship with Your Baby's Father

- Be aware that your child will always be a link between you and the father—but not necessarily the link you envision. If you have unresolved issues with the father, seek counseling before the child is born.
- Seek legal counsel if you can't agree on what the father's role will be. Learn about the laws in your state and protect your rights and those of your child. Even if this person is the last man on earth you'd like to raise your child, all fathers have rights in every state.
- Don't consider refusing to give your child's father access to your child just because he didn't want to get married. Punishing the father by refusing to let him in your child's life will hurt your child more than your ex.

Even if you are absolutely certain that it is best to have your child without a father, don't be surprised if your feelings fluctuate. It is natural to go through a grieving period as you let go of the traditional American dream of husband, home, and family that is so emphasized in our culture.

You will need to give up your dream of parenting this child from the beginning in the context of a loving relationship. Even though you may get married in the future, you need to grieve the loss of this dream before becoming a single parent.

You will cope with the stresses of single motherhood far more successfully if you are determined to become a single parent than if you are ambivalent about it. Mothers who plan their pregnancy and very much want a baby have an easier adjustment to motherhood than those who accidentally become pregnant or have very mixed feelings about whether or not to become a single mother.

If you are still uncertain about becoming a single mother, I suggest you look into joining the organization called Single Mothers by Choice, which has chapters in the United States and Canada. This organization is comprised of hundreds of SMCs, as well as what they call "thinkers"—women who are *considering* single motherhood. The "thinkers" comprise almost half of the membership as more and more women are becoming aware that single motherhood is a real option but that the decision warrants considerable thought. In many chapters of Single Mothers by Choice, "thinkers" meet together and spend months deciding whether or not single motherhood is right for them. According to Jane Mattes, the founder of Single Mothers by Choice, about 50 percent of "thinkers" decide *not* to become single mothers, but members report that it was as important for them to have gone through the decision-making process and to have made a careful choice about single motherhood as it was for women who opt to try it.

Single Fathers

As our culture continues to soften sexual stereotypes, allowing men to be more open about revealing their nurturing, emotional sides, more and more men are taking a more active role in parenting. There is an increasing number of full-time single fathers, with the number doubling in the past decade. Currently almost 14 percent of all single-parent families are headed by a father. And more and more men are considering becoming single parents by choice.

In this section, we will address the concerns of single men who are contemplating fatherhood. While many of your concerns will be similar to a single mom's, single fathers have some special considerations. I will discuss these, as well as provide questions and exercises to help you make your decision.

Having fathers as primary caretakers is certainly not new. Because of the high incidence of maternal death in childbirth prior to the twentieth century, we can only assume that even in extended-family situations, there were not enough women to carry on child care. Fathers were undoubtedly much more involved in the nurturing and care of their children than they were until relatively recently.

In a number of other cultures, fathers are not relegated to baby-sitter status, nor is their ability to be primary caretakers as readily dismissed as in our own. In fact, in some societies, men are so involved with fathering that their bodies and psyches may undergo dramatic changes before the birth of their children.

Can a Single Father Adequately Parent?

Not only is there a history of men being nurturers, but we have evidence, even in our own culture, that men nurture, interact with, and rear their children competently.

Anthropologists and ethologists have suggested that the very nature and appearance of the human infant elicits powerful nurturing responses in both men and women. Erik Erikson has credited the profound helplessness of the human infant as the force evoking nurturing responses from both men and women.

These same researchers have also concluded that there are innate biological mechanisms over and above breast-feeding that produce the female's superior attunement to her baby and that these mechanisms ultimately determine mother's greater involvement with her child.

But this is not borne out by newly discovered facts. In 1978, Michael Lamb, a developmental psychologist and researcher into the role of the father in the development of the child, decided to study this supposed "biological superiority" of women. Men and women volunteers were shown a videotape of a crying, obviously distressed infant, followed by another tape of a comfortable, cooing baby. The response of the male's nervous and circulatory systems to the tape of the upset infant—i.e., quickened pulse rate, increased rate of respiration, overall alertness of the senses—and the subsequent relaxation response to the comforted infant was indistinguishable from that of the female. Researchers concluded that social determinations outweighed biological influences (which are undoubtedly present) in shaping the sensitivity of mothers and fathers to their babies' needs.

There are, of course, important differences in the way women and men parent. Developmental psychologists have studied first-time parents and found intriguing, important differences in the way fathers and mothers handle their children. Mothers picked up their babies and held them intimately close to their neck and breasts, handling and often talking to them in a gentle, soft, low-keyed manner. Fathers seemed to always want to *do* something with their babies when they picked them up. They were playful and provocative, tickling and rough-housing, somewhat more with their sons than their daughters, though not in every case. These findings were later expanded to include the observation that fathers used more play and games in general than did mothers.

These findings were further expanded when Henry Biller, another developmental psychologist, began a series of studies in 1974 to examine a growing hunch that mothers and fathers interacted quite differently when their babies tried to explore the environment. He observed men encouraging their babies' curiosity and urging them to attempt to solve intellectual and physical challenges, persistently fostering their child's sense of mastery over the outside world, functioning as a kind of "socializer/coach."

The bottom line seems to be that the father's involvement has measurable positive effects in its own right on the development of the child.

In general, single fathers are no different from single mothers in terms of needing to set up a support system that will provide both their child and themselves much-needed separation from one another, as well as outside interests, influences, and guidance. Fathers should seek out nurturing females who will become an important part of their child's life. Most important, those with a female child will need to involve her in activities with other girls and find females who can act as surrogate mothers for their child, so the child has friends and role models to aid in the process of forming her identity.

Before considering becoming a single father, refer back to earlier sections in this book that are dedicated to single parenting in general. Make sure your lifestyle is conducive to parenting and that you are emotionally in a place to be able to handle all the stresses of parenthood, including the added pressure of needing to counter any negative comments from family and friends.

Another major concern about single fathers is the question of sexual abuse. Many fear that men simply cannot be trusted around children without the watchful eye of the mother and that activities like changing a diaper, bathing, and dressing a child, particularly a female child, are open invitations to child sexual abuse by the father. This is a valid concern, particularly for those fathers who were sexually abused themselves as children. Male victims of childhood sexual abuse are far more likely to continue the cycle of abuse by becoming sexual perpetrators themselves than are female victims. In fact, the risk is so high that I would discourage you from becoming a single father if you have a history of sexual abuse.

For those fathers who were not sexually abused, there is good news. One of the most dramatic findings in the research into father infant care revealed that whether the child is the father's or someone else's, if a man is involved in the physical care of his child before the age of three, there is a dramatic reduction in the probability that the man will be involved later in life in the sexual abuse of children in general as well as his own. (See Hilda Parker and Seymour Parker, "Cultural Rules, Rituals, and Behavior Regulation," *American Anthropologist* [86: 3, 1984] and Hilda Parker and Seymour Parker, "Father-Daughter Sexual Child Abuse: An Emerging Perspective," *American Journal of Orthopsychiatry.*)

One explanation of this is that the humanization of both father and child inherent in such activity creates a strong barrier against later exploitation of that intimacy. This may explain why mothers, even those who were themselves sexually abused as children, so seldom sexually abuse their own children.

While men may deal with discipline differently and appear to be less "emotional," they are just as proud of their children as women and they worry as fervently over their children. Although our culture does not encourage men to express the depth of their feelings as easily or as passionately as women, rest assured that the emotions men feel about fatherhood are as strong as women feel about motherhood. If you want to experience the joys of parenthood and feel, as many women do, that you just don't want to wait for Ms. Right any longer, you have every right to consider single parenthood.

Although you certainly can go the route of finding a female friend or lover who will agree to bear your child, this process will be more complicated than when a female chooses to be a single parent. After all, a woman only needs the sperm of the father, while you will need to find a woman to actually carry your baby for nine months and go through labor with the baby. Not only will very few women agree to go through such a complicated, time-consuming process, but fewer still will be able to go through it without becoming emotionally attached to the child.

Unless you already know a woman who has agreed to become impregnated by you, I suggest you look into adoption instead. Single-parent adoptions are becoming more acceptable, although there is still a great deal of resistance to allowing a single man to adopt. Your chances for successful adoption increase tremendously, however, if you are open to adopting handicapped, multiracial, or older children. These children desperately need a loving parent and a good home. If you feel you can handle the added stress and burden of caring for these children with special needs, it may be that you will be a perfect match.

Single parenting will demand everything you've got—all your strength, courage, persistence, and patience. At the same time, it can make you more than you ever dreamed possible—stronger, more courageous, more tolerant, and more patient. The triumphs and challenges are entwined—almost on a daily basis. You may relish the freedom to make decisions unimpeded by conflict with the other parent, yet at the same time feel the burden of having to make all the decisions alone. You may feel deeply lonely, even though you have hardly a waking minute to yourself. You may feel blessed to witness the beauty of a blossoming child and yet mourn the absence of a partner to share it with. For all these reasons, it is important to carefully consider all of the points discussed as you make your determination about whether being a single parent is right for you.

Part II

Are You Ready

for Parenthood?

SIX

Baby Time? Deciding Whether You Are Ready

WHILE THIS BOOK will help potential parents decide whether to have a child or not, the primary focus is on helping you to decide whether you are *ready* at this time to become a parent. Research shows that 90 percent of all couples who can have children do so, so my emphasis is on *preparing* potential parents for parenthood by informing them how their life will be different once they become parents. By helping you discover and work through potential problems ahead of time and by helping you decide whether you need to wait awhile, I hope to help you make an informed, confident decision about parenthood.

Even if you are certain you want to become a parent, you may not be sure you are ready to do so at this time. One of the most important issues surrounding the parenthood decision is the question of whether this is the right *time* to be having a baby. Although your biological clock may be ticking and you may be receiving a great deal of pressure from well-meaning friends and family, as well as being bombarded by the current "baby craze" in the media, you can't afford to base your decision on these pressures. Instead, the decision needs to be made on the basis of whether you are prepared at this time to become a parent. Becoming a parent for the first time is so stressful and requires such commitment that you must be financially, physically, and, most important, emotionally ready for it.

Questions: Is the Timing Right for You to Be Considering Parenthood?

The following are some important questions to ask yourself concerning the timing of your parenthood decision:

- Am I in good health, both emotionally and physically? Am I emotionally stable enough to withstand the stress and changes that come with a new baby? What about my partner?
- Is this a good time in our relationship for us to have a child? Is our relationship strong and stable enough to withstand the changes and turmoil that will ensue from bringing a new person into our relationship?
- Are we (or you—if you are single) financially stable enough to handle the additional expenses of having and caring for a child?
- Do I have job or professional security? What about my partner? What will having a baby mean to my career? Can I afford to take my focus off my career for the next several years while we (or I) get pregnant, give birth, and focus on getting our child off to a good start?
- Do I have enough time and energy to devote to parenting? Can I handle both the demands of my job and a child?

- Do I have a close family or a supportive network of friends?
- Do I have good health insurance?
- For women: Is my self-esteem high enough to cope with the changes that will occur to my body (if you give birth to your baby) during and after pregnancy?

Do You Have the Time Necessary to Be a Good Parent?

Part of discovering whether this is the right time for you to become a parent is for you to look at just how much *time* you actually have to devote to parenting. As you have no doubt heard, parenting is a full-time job, yet most of us do not have the luxury of having it be our *only* job.

You've heard all the stories about how much of your time having a child takes in terms of daily maintenance and so on. I'll address this issue myself in Part III. But for now, I'd like you to get a bird's-eye view of how much time, energy, and planning goes into *preparing* to have a child. The following is a suggested timetable for making preparations for bringing a child into your life.

2–3 MONTHS
- Choose a doctor, midwife, hospital.

4 MONTHS
- Notify your employer. Discuss your plans regarding your job and your pregnancy and discuss whether you intend to continue working after the birth.
- Start buying maternity clothes.
- Start thinking about child care. If you locate a good place, it's not too early to reserve a spot for your child.
- Sign up for prenatal classes.

5 MONTHS
- Start preparing the nursery.
- Start shopping for furniture and miscellaneous baby equipment.

6 MONTHS
- Order furniture to ensure its arrival before your delivery.
- Arrange for any help you may need when you are first home with baby.

7 MONTHS
- Make final preparations for nursery, finishing all painting, papering, and so on.
- Select your pediatrician. Interview potential candidates, then notify the one you've chosen, so he or she will be available when your baby arrives.
- Finalize all preparations for your maternity leave. Find and train your replacement and discuss plans with clients, staff, and so on. Start winding down your workload.
- Make final choices regarding your care at home after the delivery.
- Start childbirth classes.

8 MONTHS
- Complete all projects you've started for the baby. The room should now be ready and waiting.
- Stock up on food, freeze extra meals.
- Discuss division of chores and responsibilities with your mate (if you have one).
- Pack a suitcase in preparation for the delivery.
- Have announcements ordered or purchased.

9 MONTHS
- Stop working.
- Spend time alone with your mate (if you have one). Enjoy your last few moments of calm before the storm.

As you can see, before you even have your baby (or adopt your child), you will be focusing a great deal of time preparing for him or her (or them). Do you have enough time to adequately prepare for your child? If not, can you free up the time? If the answer to these questions is no, if you do not even have enough time to *prepare* for a child, you are certainly not ready to bring a child into your life.

Not only will all these preparations take time, they will take energy, money, and freedom. Many people realize, once they begin to plan for a child, that the way their life is presently set up is not conducive to having a child. If, for example, your work requires a twenty-four-hour-a-day involvement (such as being on call or owning your own business), you may need to consider changing careers or jobs. Would it be a relief to have a less-pressured work situation or would you feel a great loss, which in turn could become resentment toward your child?

If you have a high-powered, demanding, or otherwise stressful job, you may not have the time or energy necessary to raise a child. Although you may yearn for a child, think about how much time you actually spend at home versus how much time you spend at work. If you tend to work long hours, often not getting home before seven or eight at night, it would be unfair of you to consider having a child. You would not be around enough to give your child the time and attention he or she will need in order to grow up to be a well-adjusted, secure, happy adult. For even if you can afford a nanny or live-in child care, no one can give a child the special attention that only his or her parents can provide.

Even those who don't work long hours but have very demanding jobs need to consider carefully whether they will have the energy required to be a good parent. If you come home early from work but then spend a great part of your evenings and weekends doing job-related tasks, such as making phone calls or working on reports, you will not have the time and energy required to be a good parent. The same holds true of those who tend to fret and obsess about their jobs in their so-called "off-hours," as my client Ashley does:

"I desperately want a child, but in all fairness, my job is so all-consuming that I wouldn't have the time and energy to give to my child what she or he would need. I work long hours and even when I'm not working, I'm constantly planning and trying to come up with solutions for problems. I realize, after thinking about it, that I'd just be too preoccupied to be a good parent. My job requires my full attention and the truth is, I can't afford not to give it my all. I had to work hard to get where I am and there are plenty of other people who'd love to push me out of the way."

Questions: Do You Have the Energy to Be a Good Parent?

1. How do you feel at the end of the workday? Exhausted? Ready to take on the world with energy to burn?

2. What do you normally do after work? Go to the gym? Go for happy hour with friends? Come home and collapse on the couch?

3. What about weekends? Do you have lots of energy or do you need the weekend to recuperate from the work week and prepare for the upcoming one?

4. Do you pack your weekends with leisure-time activities, family and friends, and charity work?

5. Do you often feel like you don't have enough time and energy to get everything done?

If you find yourself exhausted at the end of the day or the end of the week, adding a child to your life obviously won't help. And it is unfair of you to bring a child into your life if you don't have the energy to be a good parent. On the other hand, if you have energy to burn and love packing your leisure time with activities, you will more than likely have the required energy for parenting. Just realize that you may have to curtail some of your current activities in order to devote needed time for your child.

Is Your Lifestyle Conducive to Child-rearing?

Some lifestyles are more conducive to child-rearing than others. Obvious examples of lifestyles that are *not* conducive to children are:

- households where both parents work long hours and have little time to devote to their children
- households where there is a great deal of fighting between parents
- households where one partner is emotionally or physically abusing the other
- households where there is a great deal of drinking or drug-taking
- households where one or both partners are compulsive gamblers, compulsive or excessive shoppers, or who are engaged in any kind of behavior that risks their livelihood and their child's security

A child needs a stable, consistent environment in order to feel safe and secure. The above situations all create the opposite: chaos, confusion, and disruption.

A special word to those who have a tendency to use alcohol or drugs to reduce stress. There is a strong possibility that you will increase your use when you become overwhelmed with the stresses of parenthood. For this reason, it is important that you assess your alcohol and drug consumption now. The time to spot a developing problem is before a child is depending on you. If you are not sure if your drinking or drug use is a problem, have a consultation with a therapist who specializes in addictions.

EXERCISE: Assessing How Your Lifestyle Will Affect Your Child and Vice Versa

1. What is most important to you in life? Success? Love? Security? Adventure? Creativity? How do you see this being affected by having a child?

2. What kind of social life do you have now? How do you imagine your social life will be affected by having a child? How much of your social life are you willing to curtail in order to take care of a child?

3. Do you need or desire more education in order to improve or enhance your life or advance your career? Would having a child interfere with this goal? Could you go to school and take care of a child? Could you afford to do both?

4. Do you live in an area that is conducive to raising children? If not, are you willing to relocate to another area that is more conducive, has better schools, more families, and so on? How far are you willing to commute to your job? Could you make a move without becoming resentful or feeling deprived?

5. Are you and your partner ready to devote the greatest portion of your time for the next eighteen to twenty years to raising a child? Are there other things you want to do that seem more important?

If, after completing these questions, you realize that there are still a lot of goals you wish to strive for or compromises you're not willing to make, maybe now is not the right time for you to become a parent. Give yourself some time to complete some of your goals before once again considering parenthood.

Can You Afford to Have a Child?

Still another major concern is whether a couple or an individual can afford to have a baby at this time. This includes making certain that there is an adequate support system set up (friends, relatives, caretakers) and that there are enough financial resources to adequately care for the baby under any circumstance.

Even the cost of daily child maintenance can be overwhelming. For example, the packages of Huggies or Pampers a baby goes through every three or four days cost approximately $10–$14; baby clothes and shoes he outgrows every few months cost anywhere from $20–$40 if he is one year old and $30–$50 if he is two. On the average, his new winter coat costs up to $50; his stroller anywhere from $100–$300. Depending on where you live, his visits to the pediatrician can cost $35–$100. If his mother continues to work, child-care costs can run as high as $25,000 a year in some cities.

In addition to everyday expenses, such as clothes, food, and medical and dental expenses, you will need to set aside money for dance, music, or sports lessons, summer camps, vacations, private schools, and eventually college, as well as for emergencies and insurance.

Another consideration is to look at what other demands there are on your income presently and in the future. Many of us today fall into what is called the "sandwich" generation, caught between taking care of elderly parents while still raising small children of our own. If you have elderly parents, will you be called upon to help them financially in the next few years or are there other members of the family who will take on this responsibility? If your parents need your hands-on help on a daily or weekly basis or need your financial assistance, this will take away from your ability to care for your child.

If you are uncertain whether you can actually afford a child at this time, spend a weekend pricing various baby and child items in your area and put together a mock budget. This will help you make a realistic assessment.

Are You Ready to Become a Single Parent?

Even though you may have determined that you are a good candidate for this type of parenting, now may or may not be a good time for you to become a parent. Therefore, the next question to consider is whether you are adequately prepared for single parenthood at this time. While we addressed this question somewhat in previous chapters, the following questions are more issue-specific and will be helpful in determining your readiness.

1. Have you accomplished all the personal and career goals that are essential to your feeling good about yourself and your life or are there some things you still want or need to do before having a baby?

2. Do you have an understanding as to why you are not with a partner at this point in your life? Have you thought about how this will affect your relationship with your child?

3. Are you clear about which of your needs can and will be met by a child and which can only be fulfilled by a mate?

4. Can you arrange your life in such a way that you can be assured of a supportive environment for yourself and your child? Does it include a network of support people (friends, relatives, neighbors, and so on) and a support system with your community (schools, church, synagogue, or other house of worship, place of employment, and so on) that you can count on to help you at difficult times? No one can raise a child completely alone. In order to be able to raise a child successfully as a single person, it is vitally important for you to create an extended family.

5. Are you in a reasonably secure financial position to support yourself and a child? In addition to having enough money to cover daily expenses, you will need to have a cushion of at least six months' income in savings so that you and your child are protected in the event that you lose your job or become seriously ill. In addition, life and health insurance are essentials for single parents in particular.

6. Have you budgeted for all aspects of childbearing and child care, including donor insemination if you are going that route? Make sure you also include insurance and necessary legal provisions for your child should something happen to you.

7. Are you prepared for the strong possibility that the baby of your dreams, the baby that you fantasize about, may not be the baby you end up with? Can you be flexible enough to accept whatever baby you give birth to or adopt? Are you strong enough to deal with the possibility that your baby may have physical problems or a learning disability?

8. Have you decided what the role of the father (or mother) will be? Before your child is born, you should consider the financial and emotional aspects of the other parent's involvement—if any. Does he want his name on the birth certificate? Does he want shared custody? Does he want to play daddy? Issues such as these should be cleared up *before* the baby is born. In some cases, it is best to seek legal advice.

9. Are you prepared for any negative remarks from friends and family? It is important that you think over carefully what you will tell family and friends and that you know how to handle people's offhand comments.

10. Have you decided how you will explain your choice to be a single parent to your son or daughter? You should be able to present to your child a positive view of your family situation and be able to answer any and all questions openly and honestly. If you cannot do this, you may not be ready for single parenthood.

11. How do you feel about your decision? Do you feel clear and strong about it or do you have ambivalent feelings? Are you experiencing feelings of shame, guilt, or fear? While it is natural for you to experience fear and to have misgivings from time to time, if you are feeling shame or guilt, you will undoubtedly pass this on to your child.

If you have decided you are, in fact, ready to become a single parent, you will still need a considerable amount of support. If you are a woman, I suggest you read the book *Single Mothers by Choice* by Jane Mattes. This book will help you with those issues that are of particular interest to single mothers— including tips on how to get through the postpartum period alone and how to handle the "daddy" issue once your child begins to ask questions.

In addition, I suggest you join the organization called Single Mothers by Choice (SMC) that I mentioned in an earlier chapter. (Please see Appendix II for information on how to contact a chapter near you.) There are approximately two thousand members and more than twenty local chapters in the United States and two in Canada. There are some basic questions and concerns that all single mothers share, no matter what their background, such as: "How can I do the best job of parenting?" "How do I manage the double role of single parent?" Talking with other single mothers will provide you with some of these answers.

For Couples: When One Is Ready and the Other One Isn't

For those in a relationship, parenthood obviously becomes a decision that both partners should have equal say in. Unfortunately, in many situations, it is difficult for partners to agree as to whether this is the right time to have a baby or even whether they should have a baby at all. The following information, exercises, and questions will help those of you who are a couple sort out your differences, become more clear as to what each person really wants, and help you reach a mutually agreed upon decision.

More often than not, it is the woman in a relationship who is the first to decide she is ready to become a parent. And it is often the man who hangs back with excuses for waiting or who refuses to even discuss it.

Many women are propelled into a state of readiness for parenthood by their biological clocks. Some don't want to be "old" parents, and others worry about the potential difficulties of getting pregnant or having a child with a birth defect since the incidence of children with birth defects increases with the age of the mother. Carla, a woman I interviewed for the book, told about her experience:

"We needed to decide whether to start a family or not and to do it soon. It had been on our minds for a long time. We knew we wanted to have children eventually, but there always seemed to be time. Then one day I realized I was thirty-three and that time was running out."

Some women feel added pressure to convince their partner to "get ready" to become a parent because they fear they will soon be too old to have a child, as was the case with Lynn:

"I got married late in life—I was thirty-eight. I'd had a full life by then, I'd had lots of love affairs, been to a lot of parties, and had done a lot of traveling. By the time I got married, I really felt like settling down and starting a family. But my husband Frank is six years younger than me and he isn't quite ready for all that. I'd be more willing to wait if I didn't feel the tick, tick of my biological clock. Frank understands my time pressure, but I'm concerned about the fact that he isn't ready. I don't want to pressure him, but what do I do with the pressure I feel?"

In most cases, those women who are faced with reluctant husbands eventually get them to agree. For some, the task is relatively easy—their strong commitment is enough to convince their partner.

Cynthia, a thirty-six-year-old commercial artist, got married at thirty-five for the first time. "As soon as Max and I became engaged, I started talking about children. He was neutral about the idea, except that he thought we should wait awhile. But as time went on, he began changing his mind. I think it was because he knew how much I love children and I was absolutely certain it would make our life so much better to have them."

Sometimes, however, a partner's ambivalence or fear contains a warning that should not be ignored. Annette's husband was initially adamant about not wanting to have children. He'd come from an abusive family and did not want to risk becoming abusive himself. "I understood his fears, but I knew Blake would be a wonderful father and I told him so. When our friends started having children and when I saw him interacting with them, I was even more certain about it. Finally, he relented."

It took much longer before Bonnie's husband Carl turned around. He kept adding to his list of what he wanted to accomplish before they had children. But Bonnie was relentless. She talked about having children constantly, pressuring him to change his mind. She even resorted to accusing him of being selfish because he wasn't willing to do something that he knew would make her happy.

While women are often successful at convincing their partners to have children, this doesn't mean it is recommended. It is unfair to both partners—and most of all to their potential offspring—to have children unless both parents are absolutely ready. In Cynthia and Max's situation, it turned out that even though Max had been neutral and it took Cynthia's enthusiasm about children to turn the tide, the end result was positive. Although he hadn't initially been "ready," he became so by the time their first baby was born. Max discovered he loved having children and wanted to have more right away.

But the results were less positive for Annette and Blake

and Bonnie and Carl. It turned out that although Blake tried very hard to be a good father, he couldn't overcome his childhood abuse. When their son Jason entered the "terrible twos" and started actively exploring his environment and saying no to every request, Blake lost patience with him very quickly and began striking him on the bottom. Annette tried to explain to Blake that Jason was just being a normal toddler and that he shouldn't scold or hit him, but Blake insisted they needed to teach Jason to mind. By the time Jason was four, Blake was completely out of control, frequently yelling at him, calling him names, carrying around a belt, and threatening to "teach him a lesson." Although Blake recognized he was acting just like his abusive father, he couldn't change his behavior. Both realized they had made a mistake by having a child.

Unfortunately, Bonnie and Carl came to the same painful conclusion. As it turned out, Carl resented Bonnie for pressuring him into becoming a parent and this resentment grew once the baby was born and their lives became completely focused on her. "I just wasn't ready to devote all my time and attention to a baby," Carl told me. "I felt shortchanged, like my youth was suddenly gone and along with it all my chances for having fun." When their child was less than six months old, Bonnie and Carl filed for divorce.

If one of you is ready and the other is not, there are positive strategies you can use to help you reach a middle ground. Neither partner should be pressured into changing their mind, especially if they have strong feelings one way or the other. If one partner is neutral, as with the case of Cynthia and Max, one person's enthusiasm can make a positive difference. But if one partner has strong feelings against having a child at this time, no amount of enthusiasm is going to make them change their feelings. While they may give in to your pressure, they are really doing it against their will, so you are setting the stage for future resentment.

Instead of pressuring your partner, try establishing an agenda of things that must be done before you consider having a child. Many couples have found that as they check off each item, one by one, they feel more and more ready, as was the case with Prisilla and Dean:

"I originally thought Dean was just making up excuses for not wanting a child yet, but after we'd made up our list, I realized there really were things we needed to do before we were emotionally and financially ready to become parents. It took us over two years to accomplish all the things on our list and by that time we really were ready."

EXERCISE: Your Agenda

1. Together with your partner, sit down and write separate lists of goals you would like to meet before becoming a parent, tasks you would like to accomplish, or changes in your life you'd like to make.

2. Each of you should now prioritize your list, making it clear which items are the most important goals to meet.

3. Share your lists with one another, making certain you don't judge one another's lists or try to talk each other out of the importance of any particular item.

4. Work on a third list that will include not only the most significant items from each of your lists but goals you share as a couple.

This exercise will serve several purposes. First of all, instead of feeling pressured and misunderstood, your partner will feel that his or her concerns are being heard and taken seriously. Second, although you may not be aware of it, you too may have goals and tasks you would like to accomplish before settling down and devoting your time and energy to raising a child. Third, by honoring one another's lists and making a joint list, you will be doing your relationship a big favor. As you know, good communication is vital to establishing and maintaining a healthy relationship. Finally, by completing your agendas before having a child, you both will be far more ready to become parents and, in particular, to become good parents who are willing and able to devote yourselves to child-rearing without resentment.

On the other hand, you may discover from examining your lists that one or both of you is nowhere near being ready to have a child. You may have so many interests and goals or your goals may be so all-consuming that you simply do not have the time to devote to child-rearing. If this is the case, it is better you know this now instead of trying to force yourself or your partner into doing something you aren't ready for or, more important, before having a child.

If your partner continually adds to his list and seems to be looking for the "perfect time" to have a child, it may be that he or she will never be ready. "It seemed like it was one thing after another with Nelson," Jill told me during one of our sessions. "First, he said he needed to get a promotion at work, then we had to save money for a house. Now he says he wants us to travel first because we won't have a chance later. I keep telling him that he's just looking for an excuse. Things are never going to be perfect, so we should just start trying to have a baby and see what happens."

But Jill was missing something. While she may have been right about Nelson looking for excuses, the fact remained that he was sending the message that he wasn't ready.

Nelson had refused to come into counseling earlier, fearing that it would be two against one—that I would side with Jill and accuse him of making up excuses. But when Jill told him that I had encouraged her to stop pressuring him, he finally accepted her invitation into couples counseling so they could explore whether they were, in fact, ready to have a child.

As it turned out, underneath all of Nelson's excuses was a deep fear of having to be responsible for a child.

"It's taking me a long time to grow up and, in some ways, I'm still a kid. Jill knows this about me, so I'm surprised she would even think I'd be ready to be a father. I think she wants a baby so much that she's just blind to everything else. But I know. I still have a lot of maturing to do."

Armed with the knowledge gained from discovering Nelson's actual agenda, both Jill and Nelson could tackle the real issue—not the excuses.

As you have seen, determining whether you are ready to be a parent involves assessing your time availability, your level of energy, your financial resources, your lifestyle, and your emotional readiness.

If you are in a relationship, the following chapter will provide you with still more information that will help you decide whether your relationship is ready for a child.

SEVEN

For Couples: Is Your Relationship Ready for a Child?

WHEN YOU ARE in a relationship, not only must both people be ready to become parents, but the relationship itself needs to be ready for a child. This means that your relationship must be able to withstand the pressures and strains placed upon it by bringing a new person into it. A very new relationship, a relationship that is undergoing a transition of some kind, or a relationship that is full of conflict often buckles under the strain of a first child.

Most couples are aware that having a baby will bring new worries, responsibilities, and financial pressures as well as new joys and gratifications, but few understand just how much their relationship will change. While most couples imagine a new baby will bring them closer together, initially a child often has the opposite effect. A new baby doesn't tend to bring a couple closer together as much as create new stresses in the relationship and accentuate those differences that exist between partners.

For this reason, deciding whether your relationship is ready for a child involves discovering exactly how having a baby affects a relationship and whether your particular relationship is up for the challenge. This includes everything from how a new baby affects a couple's sex life, to how it changes a couple's communication, to how each person's priorities will change once the baby arrives.

Questions: Is Your Relationship Ready for a Child?

1. Have the two of you had enough time together to really get to know one another?

2. Have you had time enough together to work out any sexual problems?

3. Have you done many of the romantic things you've always dreamed of (i.e., a romantic honeymoon or vacation to a tropical paradise)?

4. Are you ready to bring another person into your relationship, to have your present relationship change into something else?

5. Is your relationship going through a transition, such as learning to communicate with each other differently?

6. Is one of you going through a major transition, such as a new job?

7. Is one of you under a great deal of stress right now, such as having to take care of a sick parent, pressure on the job, or having to cope with a personal failure?

8. Is your relationship fraught with conflicts and disagreements? Do you argue continuously or have you been unable to resolve some major issues?

If you answered no to more than two of items 1–4 or yes to any of items 5–8, you may need to give your relationship time before subjecting it to the stresses of bringing a child into it. If you are already experiencing conflicts in your relationship, these need to be worked out before you bring the complications into the relationship that a child creates.

In this chapter, I will discuss some of the most problematic differences in how women and men are affected by the arrival of a new baby and how to discover them *before* deciding whether to become parents. For example, research tells us that men and women often feel, think, and perceive in very different ways. Few experiences in life highlight these fundamental male/female differences as sharply as the birth of a child. Even couples who think of themselves as like-minded often find their priorities and needs diverging dramatically when they become parents.

The Transition to Parenthood

In their book *The Transition to Parenthood: How a First Child Changes a Marriage*, Jay Belsky, Ph.D., and John Kelly outline the research findings of the Penn State Child and Family Development Project pertaining to the effect a child has on the marital relationship. The study, which began in the early 1980s, found that men and women experience the transition to parenthood in such dramatically different ways that in most marriages, not one but two transitions develop: a his and a hers.

Her Transition

According to Belsky and Kelly, while men and women become parents at the same time, they don't become parents in the same way. Most of the profound changes that occur during the transition, especially in its early phases, happen to the woman—and that makes her transition much more tumultuous than her husband's. A great deal of this upheaval, of course, is positive. So positive, in fact, that many women describe it as ecstasy. "The realization that one has created life and the joy that comes with it is beyond compare," one woman told me. The love affair that a mother has with her baby only adds to her feeling of ecstasy. Another mother told me, "I never dreamed I could love anyone like this."

Some of the upheaval is not so positive. In the weeks and months following the baby's birth, many women suffer from chronic fatigue and exhaustion and some suffer from anxiety, depression, and low self-esteem. To some extent, these conditions are related. Fatigue and physical weakness create a vulnerability to unpredictable mood swings. But a great deal of a new mother's emotional upheaval arises from her unique relationship to the baby. Some women find their feelings toward their child to be so powerful they become all-consuming. They can't think of anything but the baby and sometimes have a difficult time removing themselves from his or her presence. Doubts about their competence as mothers also plague new mothers.

Worries about self are another common feature of the mother's transition. A University of Minnesota study indicated that new mothers also worry about the physical changes the baby has produced in her. "Loss of figure" and "general unhappiness about appearance" were two of the top five transition complaints of the study.

His Transition

The father's transition is not free of upheaval. There is some evidence that new fathers worry even more than new mothers about the effect a new baby will have on their work and their financial situation. And to varying degrees, new fathers also worry about fatigue, intrusive in-laws, chores, and what their wives are enduring.

On the whole, though, the male transition is more even-keeled. Paternal love is slower to develop, sometimes taking weeks and months. Perhaps because of this, it is also easier to control. There are also fewer lows in the father's transition. While a new mother's stress levels continue to rise throughout the first year after a baby's birth, new fathers stress tends to level off after the first month. But there are fewer highs too. In a recent survey, only 1 percent of new fathers described their baby's first step as a "big thrill," compared with 17 percent of new mothers.

EXERCISE: Your Concerns

1. What are you most worried about concerning having a baby? Consider all the following:
- changes in your relationship
- financial concerns
- the intrusion of in-laws
- whether you will be a good parent or not
- whether or not you actually *like* children

2. What do you think are your partner's concerns about having a baby?

3. Are your concerns similar or different from your partner's? Now ask your partner to complete this exercise to compare notes.

What happens to a marriage (or other strong union) during the transition is ultimately the result of the discoveries a couple makes about one another as they try to resolve their differences. For example, they may discover unrecognized capacities for self-sacrifice, understanding, empathy, and compassion that bring them closer together. Or they may discover unrecognized tendencies of stubbornness and selfishness that can create distance between them.

Common Topics of Dispute

New parents fight about many things, but they tend to fight most about the following five issues: division of labor, money, work, their relationship (who is responsible for the wedge that has been created between them), and their social life. According to the authors of *The Transition to Parenthood*, these five issues are so important that those couples who manage to resolve them in a mutually satisfactory way generally become happier with their marriages, whereas those who do not become unhappier. Unfortunately, a combination of biology and upbringing have conspired to make men and women see these issues very differently.

Chores and Division of Labor

On the whole, men and women agree that this is the biggest stressor of the transition. Compared with their fathers and grandfathers, men today are notably more involved in baby and household chores. Studies show that, on average, thirty years ago a man devoted eleven hours per week to home and baby, while today he devotes fifteen or sixteen hours. But this increase has not significantly alleviated the burden of new mothers. Even in a home where a woman works full-time, studies found that her contributions to child care, such as diapering, feeding, and bathing, often exceed her husband's by nearly 300 percent. In addition, the new mother's contribution to household chores also increases during the transition, usually by about 20 percent.

Consequently, many new mothers feel that they don't get the help and support they need—even when their husband is involved with home and child. Part of the answer to this conundrum lies in the fact that men and women perceive their contribution to home and baby differently from one another.

Women tend to gauge what their husband does against what they do and because what a man does looks small when evaluated by this measuring stick, women often end up unhappy and disgruntled. Men, on the other hand, usually measure their contribution to chores against what their fathers did. And because their fifteen to sixteen hours per week represent a 30 to 40 percent increase over what their fathers did, they often feel very good about themselves.

Men's perceptions of who does what are also influenced by the fact that, at least temporarily following the birth of a baby, men often become their family's sole breadwinner. Because this is a role men have been taught to equate with parenting, fulfilling it not only makes new fathers feel like they are satisfying their parental obligation, it also makes the 20 percent they do at home seem like 200 percent to them.

Conflicts over the division of labor are further increased when a man does not get the gratitude he feels he is entitled to for doing more than his father did in his day. If his attempts are met with disappointment or emotional or physical withholding on the part of his spouse, he may, in turn, feel like doing even less in the future. Worse yet, a woman's biological investment in the child may cause her to be so critical of her husband's parenting that, without intending to, she drives him away. Men who find themselves continually criticized for their inadequate diapering, bathing, and dressing skills often end up feeling conflicted. On the one hand, they know their wives do not really mean to be hurtfully critical; on another level, they feel humiliated and often conclude that the best policy is to adopt a hands-off policy when it comes to child-care chores.

The following questions will help you evaluate the current situation in your home regarding the division of labor and help you to predict future conflicts once you become parents. It will also help you as potential parents discover what your expectations of your partner are regarding child-rearing and whether you want a shared parenting experience or not. I encourage each of you to answer the questions honestly, not how you imagine your mate would answer or would want you to answer.

1. Are you satisfied with the division of labor in your household at the present time?

2. Would you like your spouse to participate more in household chores and other family responsibilities? Or are you the one who is accused of not carrying your weight?

3. Has there been a long-standing battle going on concerning who does what in your household?

4. Do you have any hope that the situation will change? If yes, what would you like to be changed the most?

5. Have either you or your partner agreed to make changes in the past but not followed through?

6. Do you and your partner have certain chores you consider "gender-specific" (i.e., "women's work" or "guy things")? Are you in agreement about these divisions? How open are you to changing this point of view?

7. Does your partner feel he or she shouldn't have to do certain chores around the house because he or she makes more money than you do?

8. Have you two discussed the division of labor once a baby is born? Are you in agreement about the following issues? Who will be primarily responsible for diapering the baby? Who will be responsible for feeding and bathing her? Who will get up with the baby at night? Who will do the dishes and the laundry?

Money Issues

Most of the disagreements new mothers and fathers have about expenses arise due to the fact that parenting changes men's and women's self-perceptions in very different ways. New fathers tend to focus their energies on conserving and enhancing financial resources, such as working longer hours to increase income and cutting back on their consumption (i.e., carrying a sack lunch to work instead of eating out). New mothers may also cut down on spending, but since they see themselves first and foremost as nurturers, their chief concern becomes the baby's well-being. This often produces economic choices that put them in conflict with their conservative-minded husbands.

A good example of this was my client Dana's decision to baby-proof the house, including putting special latches on all cabinets, replacing their glass-covered coffee table with a round-edged stone one, and having a fence built around their swimming pool. Her husband Forest, who was struggling to support the family as it was, couldn't understand why she spent money they needed for more immediate needs on things that wouldn't become hazards until the baby was two or three years old. Dana, on the other hand, felt Forest wasn't being a good father by begrudging her the money it cost to ensure their child's safety. "How can he be so stingy?" she asked me.

Money conflicts can arise even more often with those couples who both work or where both members worked prior to the baby's arrival. When men were providing most of the family's income, a mother often had to curb her spending impulses because it was money he earned that she was spending. But now that many new mothers are accustomed to having independent sources of income, they feel (within limits, of course) that they have a right to spend their money as they choose. And if they are no longer working, it is often difficult for them to transition to consulting with or deferring to a spouse regarding spending decisions. The following questions will help you evaluate your current financial situation with regards to spending and to anticipate potential problems.

1. What is the current financial climate in your house? Do you have joint checking or separate checking? Do you confer with one another about major purchases only or do you follow an agreed upon budget?

2. What are your current spending habits? Are you rather indulgent or committed to saving all you can?

3. What about your partner's spending habits? Are you often critical of how much your partner spends on items you find frivolous?

4. Do you and your partner often argue over money?

5. Have either one of you promised to change in the past but have been unable to keep that promise?

6. Who will contribute more toward the upbringing of the baby? Does that mean this person should have more of a say in making financial decisions concerning the baby?

7. How will you set spending priorities once the baby is born?

Working to create a financial strategy with which you are both comfortable will alleviate a lot of tension for you and your spouse both now and in the future.

Relationship Difficulties

A recent University of Michigan study found that the incidence of sexual intercourse drops 30 to 40 percent in the first year after the baby's arrival. And a recent *Parenting* magazine survey found that new mothers and fathers are actually twice as likely to kiss their baby as they are each other.

Fatigue is obviously partly responsible for this change. It is no secret that most new parents, especially new mothers, are just too exhausted to think about sex. Another part of the answer is that new parents tend to focus the attention and affection on their new baby that they used to direct toward one another. But the primary reason new parents touch less frequently and have less sex is that they feel less connected emotionally.

According to the findings in *The Transition to Parenthood*, one of the main reasons for this estrangement is once again differences in upbringing and biology. Most men will say that the culprit is their partner's preoccupation with the baby. While most new fathers expect the baby to become a priority in the family, many are shocked at just how little attention and affection their wives have left over for them.

Another factor adding to a man's sense of estrangement is the group of female relatives and friends who gather around the new mother. Their sudden importance as advisers and nurturers in a wife's life often causes a husband to feel unimportant and pushed aside. Mothers-in-law and sisters-in-law were found to be the number one complaint of new fathers, according to a University of Minnesota study.

Women see males' tendency to be self-focused as the chief culprit responsible for their feelings of estrangement from their husbands. According to the *Transition* study, due to upbringing and perhaps biology, a man's emotional energy and attention all too frequently tend to flow inward toward his own concerns and needs.

The association men often make between work and parenting (suddenly feeling "more responsible") can also contribute to the feelings of alienation and estrangement for a couple, as it was with Patsy and Cliff:

"Just when I needed Cliff to be home more with me and the baby, he suddenly started working longer and longer hours at work. He told me it was because he wanted to work overtime to help pay for the baby expenses and I know that feels important to him. But it's just as important for him to be here to help out and for him to bond with the baby."

How Is Your Sexual Relationship?

Knowing ahead of time about how a new baby can negatively affect your sexual relationship can help you avoid potential problems, especially if you work on your communication skills. But you don't want to *start out* with sexual problems only to have them become worse when the baby arrives. The following questions will help you to evaluate your current sexual relationship.

1. Are you satisfied with your present sexual relationship with your partner? If not, how would you like it to be different?

2. Do you believe your partner is satisfied? If not, why not?

3. Do you believe your sexual relationship has become increasingly more satisfying or increasingly less satisfying since you and your partner have been together?

4. Have you made attempts to communicate your needs to your partner? If you haven't, why have you held back?

5. If you have tried to communicate your needs, how has your partner responded? Did he or she seem open to hearing what you had to say or did your partner become defensive and hurt?

6. Do you believe your partner tries to please you and takes into consideration your needs or do you feel he or she focuses primarily on his or her own needs?

7. Has your partner made attempts to communicate his or her sexual needs to you? If so, how have you responded? Defensively or openly?

8. Do you try to please your partner and take into consideration his or her needs or do you primarily focus on your own?

9. If you could change one thing about your sexual relationship, what would it be? Do you feel you could share this with your partner? If not, why not?

10. If your partner could change one thing about your sexual relationship, what do you imagine it might be? Do you feel your partner could feel free telling you this? If not, why not?

11. Do you worry that because you aren't meeting your partner's needs, he or she will have an affair outside the marriage?

12. Do you think your partner worries about this with you? Would you ever consider having an affair if your needs weren't being met?

13. Has your partner already had an affair that you are unable to forgive?

14. Have you had an affair that your partner has been unable to forgive?

15. Does your partner have a sexual dysfunction (i.e., impotence, premature ejaculation, difficulty reaching orgasm, pain or discomfort upon penetration)? If so, how long has it been a problem? Has your partner sought professional help for the problem? If not, why not?

16. Do you have a sexual dysfunction? If so, for how long? Have you sought help for your problem? If not, why not?

17. Does your partner tend to blame you for his or her sexual problem or lack of sexual satisfaction in the relationship?

18. Do you tend to blame your partner for your sexual problem or lack of sexual satisfaction?

19. Is there any part of your partner's sexual behavior that concerns you? That you feel is unhealthy or even illegal? If there is, have you tried talking about your concerns? If yes, how has your partner responded?

20. Has your partner discussed his or her concerns about any aspect of your sexual behavior that he or she feels might be unhealthy or illegal? If so, what was your reaction?

If you discover that you and your partner have more sexual problems than you realized or if you have concerns about your partner's sexual attitudes or behavior, I suggest you discuss them with your partner. If you are afraid to do so, this is an indication that your relationship is in trouble and marital counseling is definitely in order. Although sexual problems are a common occurrence for many couples, the loaded nature of the subject matter often makes this a difficult subject to negotiate without professional guidance.

Career and Work

Between 1970 and 1990, the number of employed mothers with young children doubled, from 30 percent to 53 percent. This change in the numbers of employed mothers fueled another important change—women began to expect equality when it came to role-sharing. This expectation, in turn, led them to expect marital equality. Women today expect their partner to share emotional responsibility for their child and family and to share in career sacrifices if they are necessary. This has created yet another source of divisiveness between women and men during their transition to parenthood.

Because most males still have a lingering allegiance to certain aspects of the traditional male role, they are often psychologically and emotionally unprepared to be the full partner their wives want and expect. Unlike his father or grandfather, today's father will bathe and diaper the baby. But he, like them, often believes that chores that involve assuming emotional responsibility for home and child, such as making child-care arrangements, scheduling pediatrician's visits, and making out shopping lists, are basically a woman's work—whether she has a job outside the home or not.

Career conflicts are also common during the parenthood transition because men (or the partner who tends to make the most money or have the job with the highest prestige factor) tend to view themselves as the family's principal breadwinner and this, in turn, produces an expectation that he should not be the one to make career sacrifices. For example, the average male will agree to pick up the baby at the baby-sitter or child-care center if his wife has to work late but most still see it as her job. And even fewer men are willing to fix dinner and take over child-care responsibilities for the entire evening while their wife works late.

The following questions will address some of the issues new parents must face concerning their values regarding child-rearing, as well as those they must face when both are involved in their careers.

1. Do you believe in both parents sharing equally in the raising of their child? Or do you hold to a more traditional view that the man should be the breadwinner and the woman be the primary caretaker?

2. Are you in agreement as to who will be the primary caretaker of your child? Is one of you more willing and able to take on the role of primary caretaker than the other?

3. Will this require that this person sacrifice his or her career in order to take on this role? If so, how does he or she feel about it?

4. If both parents continue to work, do you feel the woman should still be the primary homemaker and caregiver to the child?

5. Do you believe a child raised by a mother who works will grow up to be as emotionally healthy as one whose mother stays at home?

6. Are you considering coparenting, that is, both of you sharing equally in all responsibilities surrounding the baby? Will this require sacrifices regarding both of your careers?

7. In addition to household concerns, have you considered the following issues? How will you handle taking hours off from your job? Who will take care of pediatrician appointments? Who will pick up your child from school or from the baby-sitter? Who will attend school conferences?

Emotional Support

Research also indicates that emotional involvement is another priority of most new mothers. The new mother wants to feel that, in his own way, her partner is as involved in their new family as she is. This means she wants a spouse who will sit and listen when she wants to talk about her doubts, anxieties, and frustrations; who will play with and care for the baby instead of returning him or her in ten minutes; and who will check the refrigerator to see if the family needs anything before he goes to the store.

New mothers want their husbands to understand their profound attachment to the baby and to understand why she may sometimes neglect them emotionally and physically to be with the baby. Equally important, new mothers want a spouse who understands how powerful her feelings are about the baby and how difficult these feelings sometimes are and to help her regain her emotional balance.

On the other hand, there are mothers who feel overly possessive of their child or who are fearful of having their partner take care of the child. These women would be threatened by a partner who wished to share equally in child-rearing.

The following questions will help you determine how much involvement with the baby is comfortable for each of you and what your expectations are regarding your partner's parenting style.

EXERCISE: Your Ideal Parenting Partner

1. Write a description of your idea of an ideal mother.

2. Write a description of your idea of an ideal father.

3. Make a list of the qualities you most want your partner to have as a new parent (i.e., empathy, reliability, patience, consideration, tolerance).

4. Which of these qualities does your partner now have?

5. Which of these qualities do you think is possible for your partner to obtain?

6. Make a list of the roles and tasks you would like your partner to fulfill as parent to your child.

7. Write a description of the role you imagine you will play as the mother/father of your child. Include in your description as many roles and tasks as you can imagine that you will be called upon to fulfill.

Social Isolation

In the *Transition* study, recreational activities in the form of outings to movies, restaurants, and friends' homes declined by 40 percent during the first year of the transition to parenthood. These findings tend to confirm what we already know— new parents do not tend to go out much during the first six months after their baby's birth.

New mothers tend to suffer more from isolation than new fathers, and new mothers who are staying at home for the first time suffer most of all. Work protects both men and women from the desperate kind of isolation that many new stay-at-home mothers endure, when they long for another adult to talk to. But even working parents, both men and women, complain about feeling isolated and cut off, missing their golf or racquetball games, their evenings with friends, and their vacations. Like the other major transition stresses, this one is perceived very differently by the two sexes.

Men tend to blame the couples' isolation on their wives' obsession with the baby. Grant is a typical example of this perception: "The reason we don't go out anymore is that Karen is so overprotective. She won't trust the baby to anyone except a family member and even then she's reluctant. Her mother takes care of the baby while we are both at work, so we can't ask her to baby-sit on the weekend. And my mother is too sick to take on that kind of responsibility. Even when we do find a family member to baby-sit, Karen calls home every hour, checking on the baby. Last week she told me she didn't really want to go out, that she'd rather stay home with the baby. As if I didn't already know."

Karen has her own version of the problem. "I know Grant is feeling unhappy because we hardly ever go out anymore. But I just don't think he understands how much I miss the baby while I'm at work. In the evening and on the weekend, I want to make up for lost time with the baby—I really don't want to go out. I wish he understood and frankly, I wish he felt the same."

The following questions will help you address the issue of how to deal with your social life and recreational activities once the baby is born.

1. Do you share an active social life now or is one of you more of a homebody?

2. Do you already experience conflicts over how often you go out as a couple, what kind of social activities you prefer to do together, or how often one of you likes to pursue individual activities?

3. How do you imagine having a child will affect your social life?

4. What individual activities that you currently pursue would you be willing to give up?

5. Are you willing to baby-sit so that your partner can pursue a favorite individual activity?

6. Are there couple activities that neither one of you want to forgo? If so, have you talked about instituting a "date night"?

7. Have you talked about the issue of baby-sitters and child care? Are you in agreement as to when you will first begin using baby-sitters and for what purposes?

8. Have you considered scheduling a romantic weekend away *now,* prior to the baby's arrival?

Once you both have answered all the questions in this chapter, compare your answers and begin a discussion based on your findings. I deliberately worded the questions in an impersonal way so as to illicit freer, less-censored responses, but I encourage you to turn your discussion into a personal one in which you discuss the details of your present relationship and the issues that you will need to face before bringing a child into your home.

Making a Successful Transition to Parenthood

One of the most significant findings of the *Transition* study were the factors that account for why some couples cope with the transition to parenthood more successfully than do others. They concluded that six characteristics in particular would be very important in such a passage. They were the ability to:

- surrender individual goals and needs and work together as a team
- resolve differences about division of labor and work in a mutually satisfactory manner
- handle stress in a way that does not over stress a partner or a marriage

- fight constructively and maintain a pool of common interests despite diverging priorities
- realize that however good a marriage becomes postbaby, it will not be good in the same way it was prebaby
- maintain the ability to communicate in a way that continues to nurture the marriage

According to the *Transition* study, the chief characteristic of those couples who are able to successfully make the transition to parenthood is the ability to reconcile their conflicting priorities. Husbands can do this by recognizing that their wives' need for physical and emotional support far outweighs any needs they may have and by surrendering some of their autonomy and "stepping deeper into the marriage" to provide their wives with that help and support. Wives need to recognize that their husbands' wish for more attention and affection also represent a legitimate desire and to learn how to control their feelings about the baby so they can meet their husbands at least halfway on these desires. They also need to recognize that their husbands will see the support they offer differently than they do and show them some of the gratitude they expect for their commitment to their new family.

Mutual empathy is another characteristic of those couples who successfully make the transition to parenthood successfully. The husband and wife who work at becoming attuned to one another *before* the baby comes, can resolve the inevitable conflicts that arise.

Fortunately, the two transitions to parenthood are united by a common set of gratifications. Men and women both report that parenthood makes them feel better about themselves, their parents and the larger world. Both also find the baby irresistible. Also uniting the two is a new, common set of concerns. In nearly equal degrees new mothers and fathers worry about all of the new work and financial pressures the baby creates and about how parenthood will affect their relationship with each other as well as how it will affect their work.

Honestly answering and discussing the questions in this chapter will go a long way toward discovering whether your relationship is ready to take on the responsibility of a baby. If you wish to learn more about the transition to parenthood, I recommend that you read *The Transition to Parenthood* by Jay Belsky, Ph.D., and John Kelly. (See Appendix I for more details.) The book not only details the differences between his and her transitions in far more detail than I have provided here but also explains why some couples grow closer and others grow apart.

Part III

Are You Willing

to Be a Parent?

EIGHT

Willingness Means Awareness and Commitment

WILLINGNESS INVOLVES more than desire: It involves awareness and commitment—awareness of exactly what it means to be a parent and a lifetime commitment to face all that needs to be faced and to persevere even under the most difficult of circumstances. This chapter is devoted to these two measurements of your willingness.

Awareness

Before you can truly say you are willing to be a parent, you need to know what you're getting into. You need to learn what being a parent actually entails, to know what to expect.

I will begin by asking the following series of questions regarding your willingness to have a baby. Some of these questions may seem to be obvious, things that you may have already considered, but I present them just in case you haven't considered them and also to stress the importance of these particular questions. Other questions will probably be new to you, things you haven't considered but should.

For Mothers

- Are you willing to carry an infant in your body for nine months and to gain anywhere from fifteen to forty pounds during the pregnancy?
- Are you willing to risk feeling unattractive and unsexy for at least six of those months?
- Are you willing to endure the pain of a vaginal birth or the possibility of a cesarean birth?
- Are you willing to accept the fact that your mate will be giving a great deal of love and attention to someone else?
- Are you willing to have your relationship with your partner change, including the possibility that your sex life will change?
- Are you willing to devote the first few weeks and months of your baby's life entirely to taking care of him or her?

For Fathers

- Are you willing to adjust to the physical changes that will occur to your partner's body as she carries your child (i.e., weight gain, enlarged breasts, stretch marks, increased sensitivity in the vagina)?
- Are you willing to go without sex during some part of your wife's pregnancy and for some time after the baby is born?
- Are you willing to be supportive of and faithful to your wife, even when her pregnancy causes her to become cranky and disinterested in sex?
- Are you willing to share your partner's love and attention with someone else?

- Are you willing to cope with the inevitable changes having a baby will have on your relationship?

For Single Parents

- Are you willing to accept the possibility that you may not achieve some or any of your unmet personal and career goals?
- Are you willing to endure the judgment and criticism of those who disapprove of your decision to become a single parent?
- Are you willing to accept the strong possibility that being a single parent will make your chances for finding a partner more difficult?
- Are you willing to accept the possibility that the baby of your dreams may not be the baby you end up with? That your child may not be the sex or have the temperament, personality, or talents that you had hoped for? That your child may be emotionally or physically handicapped?

For All New Parents

1. Are you willing to get only two hours of sleep at a time—or even in an entire night?

2. Are you willing to completely child-proof your house, including taking all your beautiful vases, sculpture, and antiques and putting them out of harm's way (and possibly out of sight altogether)?

3. Are you willing to have the house strewn with toys, clothes, and other children's messes?

4. Are you willing to feel absolutely overwhelmed with the knowledge that you are responsible for your child's life, safety, security, and development?

5. Are you willing to turn your house into Grand Central

Station as family, friends, and neighbors stream in to see the baby? What about later when all kids in the neighborhood flock to your house to play and have cookies and milk?

6. Are you willing to forgo personal pleasures? For example, are you willing to give up: Long leisurely baths, so you can give your new baby three or four baths a day? Quiet walks in the park, so you can spend half an hour dressing and packing up all your toddler's "equipment and supplies" for a short outing in the park before he or she throws a tantrum and must be taken home? Saturday golf games with your friends for miniature golf with an irritable seven-year-old who is an incredibly poor sport? A quiet Saturday night dinner out at a fancy restaurant for a rousing dinner at Chuck E. Cheese's?

7. Are you willing to go days without talking to an adult about something other than diaper rash or teething?

Other Considerations: Accepting the Bad Times as Well as the Good

In addition to all the above contingencies, there are also some more serious ones to consider, such as:

- What if I (we) have twins, triplets, quadruplets?
- What if the baby is born with a birth defect?
- What if something happens to my partner and I have to raise the baby all alone?
- What if I lose my job?

Willingness to be a parent involves being able to anticipate and accept the bad times as well as the good. Potential parents need to consider every stage of parenthood, from infancy to young adulthood. All too often, prospective parents tend to exaggerate the joys of parenthood while ignoring the problems and sorrows (or vice versa). In order to help you achieve the clearest focus, I present the following exercise:

1. Visualize the following images. Notice any emotions that are stirred up by each:

- a wailing, red-faced, wrinkled-up newborn
- a peacefully nursing three-month-old baby
- a cranky, teething seven-month-old
- a smiling, dimpled nine-month-old experiencing his first ice cream cone
- a grinning one-year-old with a bowl of spaghetti poured over her head
- a toddler taking his first steps
- a toddler having a temper tantrum on the floor of the supermarket
- a five-year-old reading his first book
- a six-year-old falling off his bicycle and requiring stitches
- an eight-year-old telling you you're the best mom (or dad) there is
- a thirteen-year-old saying, "You can't make me!"
- a fifteen-year-old being on the honor list for the third time
- a sixteen-year-old being arrested for drug possession
- a seventeen-year-old being caught having sex in her room
- an eighteen-year-old receiving a full scholarship to college
- a twenty-five-year-old walking down the aisle on her wedding day

2. Could you visualize each of these scenes or did you find yourself wanting to skip over some of them? Which were the most difficult to visualize? What emotions were elicited by these difficult images? Do you feel that as a parent you are prepared to accept these bad moments? If you choose not to have children, have you really considered the pleasures you'll be giving up, as well as the freedom you're maintaining?

What to Expect

In childbirth education classes, the most commonly asked questions that men and women alike ask are: "When will the baby get into a routine and sleep through the night?" "When will we be able to make love just as we did before?" But the most important question that lurks in all potential parents' minds, whether they voice it or not, is: "When will we get back to normal?" The answer to this question is—never. Your life will never be the same as before. Once a baby is born or a new child comes into your home, everything in your life changes.

Changes and Stresses on Your Relationships

Your relationships with others will undoubtedly be affected by the birth of a baby or the introduction of a new child into the home. Family and friends will see you as different and you will see yourself and them in altered ways. As a result, you may begin to behave differently toward one another, sometimes dramatically, sometimes subtly.

If you have a partner, your relationship with him or her will probably change the most. As mentioned earlier, the birth of a baby, far from deepening your understanding of one another, can often strain a relationship to the point of severing it. Studies show that the time after the birth of a baby is especially stressful for a man and a woman. A mother who is going through a difficult time emotionally will look to her partner for support, expecting him to be unfailingly strong and reliable. Simultaneously, he may be feeling helpless or anxious and get angry or retreat because he feels attacked or inadequate. She then feels rejected and unloved.

Men, even those who are loving fathers, sometimes cannot help feeling that the baby is an intruder and it is common for them to feel jealous and demanding. This often causes women to feel as if they have two babies to take care of.

Even when a man is not afraid to enter the female world of love and personal commitment, when he enjoys the baby, is sensitive to and aware of the woman's needs, and takes his full share in parenting, there is a dramatic change of scene and tempo. With a lesbian couple, there is a similar scene change, bringing opportunities for growth but also new challenges to the relationship. This is not simply due to the psychobiological impact of motherhood, with the woman's endocrine system, or with lactation—it is the same when a couple adopts a baby or when parents take over a baby who has been born to a surrogate mother. The fact is, bringing another full-time person into any relationship is going to necessitate mental, emotional, and physical adjustment and reorganization. And it happens however well a couple has prepared for parenthood. What preparation can do, however, is to help them identify problems, communicate with each other better, and enjoy the good times more.

There are major decisions to be made about where to live, jobs, income, child care and schooling, and intangible things such as shared and conflicting values, religion, and convictions about child-rearing. Once the baby has arrived, it becomes absolutely necessary to plan ahead, even for something as simple as a trip to the store.

Having to do all this thinking ahead reshapes a couple's lives. A relationship that once thrived on spontaneity, surprise, and flexibility may not flourish when there has to be so much planning. When the couple hears other people mention that they seem to be "settling down," it may set off alarms: "Are we becoming our parents?" "Am I saying goodbye to my youth?"

When a couple has been together for a while before having a baby, their once ordered pattern of existence may become reduced to chaos. If both are employed, they may have grown to depend on a certain structure for efficiency. The upheaval that a baby brings may cause both to feel they have lost control of their lives and that the baby is wrecking their relationship.

If one partner works while the other stays at home, they may find that their interests are now drastically different. The partner who is working outside comes back home at the end of the day and introduces news of the outside world that may leave the at-home partner feeling totally cut off or resentful. If the one who is employed is disengaged from most of what is going on at home, this split may become a split in the relationship that may grow wider as the mother becomes more child-centered and increasingly isolated.

Time

One of the biggest changes that comes with a new baby is that your time is no longer your own. Parents of newborns in particular feel as if time has been snatched from them. They being to feel that they will never catch up, never be able to get organized, plan ahead with confidence, to take charge of their lives again.

The ordinary divisions of time—into morning, afternoon, evenings and night, and before and after meals—often lose all meaning. In their place there seems to be a long endless list of tasks—feeding, changing, soothing and rocking, doing laundry, cleaning up, feeding again, more soothing and rocking, managing to wash yourself and change clothes if you are lucky, feeding again, carrying the baby around, putting clothes in the dryer, grabbing something to eat, picking the baby up, another feeding. There is never any point at which you can say that you are finished.

Typical tasks, such as dishwashing, increase from once or twice a day to four times, laundry from one load a week to four or five, shopping from one trip per week to three, meal preparation from twice a day to four times, and household cleaning from once a week to usually once a day.

Baby tasks add further to the workload. On average, a baby needs to be diapered six or seven times and bathed two or three times per day, soothed two or three times per night and as often as five times per day.

If you are the kind of person whose self-worth is primarily achieved by what you are able to accomplish or if you require structure in order to feel secure, having a new child in your life will be a tremendous challenge to you and may initially cause you a great deal of distress.

If you plan on returning to work either outside the home or to a home-based business, your time will get split into two different sections—work time and baby time. This may bring a sense of relief to you or may become very stressful. Baby time is still fluid and rather unformed. Work time, especially if it is in a large institution, is probably rather rigid. It may be impossible for you to switch off entirely from the baby when you are at work or you may worry and feel guilty about leaving him. When you are at home, work may begin to feel like an unreal world and you may resent being pulled away from your baby by it or you may yearn for work because you feel more confident in that section of your life.

Emotional Changes

Taking personal responsibility for a child's life often causes both women and men to become more sensitive and vulnerable, to value their own and others' lives more, to become more aware of their environment and work toward making the world a better place. But it can also cause parents to feel insecure, inadequate, and to question and assess their previous beliefs, values, and priorities.

The birth of a child can be a passage into adulthood for both sexes. Although there are other ways to mature, parents often find that parenthood confronts them with new aspects of themselves and causes them to experience the most profound and often disturbing emotions.

Because most men are less directly involved and generally involved for shorter periods of time, this maturation process can pass some of them by or be slower and more drawn out. But as a woman (or a man—if he is the primary caretaker) lives and breathes her baby for the first few months of its life, as she cleans up, soothes, rocks, and above all, as she feeds her baby, sustaining its life, she looks into the eyes of another human being who is seeing the world—seeing her—for the first time. And through the child's eyes, she sees herself anew.

WOMEN'S EMOTIONAL CHANGES

Sometimes this process forces women to ask searching questions, such as: "Is this what I want?" "Who am I?" "How did I get where I am today?" "What is going to happen in the future?"

Perhaps the most surprising and unacknowledged feeling that a woman has after giving birth have to do with grieving. For some, it is the loss of the baby inside them—the sense of closeness. A pregnant woman has never been so close to anyone else before. With the birth of the baby, she may feel very alone again.

When a woman has enjoyed pregnancy, enjoyed the attention and the feeling of specialness, the birth of her baby may cause her to feel somehow diminished in the eyes of the world. In addition, her encounter with the real baby she has borne requires her to grieve the loss of her dream baby, particularly if the baby is the wrong sex, looks entirely different from what she expected, seems to ignore her, fails to appreciate her efforts, seems to be too aggressive, or clings to her in a dependent way that she cannot tolerate.

For many women, motherhood also means losing an aspect of the self—as young, vibrant, and sexually attractive. As a result, a woman may become resentful and grieve over her lost youth.

For some women, especially those who became pregnant shortly after the start of a relationship, the birth of a baby also spells the loss of romance. Babies bring disorder and mess. A couple who believed that a baby would draw them closer may find that they are pulled apart. Intimacy is invaded.

When you become a parent, you also say goodbye to yourself as a child. This cannot be an instantaneous process and women in particular can be helped in this transition by her own mother and female friends. In many traditional cultures, other women of the tribe care for the new mother, relieve her of duties like housework, cooking, and her work in the fields. At the end of this transition period, a ceremony takes place and she emerges as a mother able to take full responsibility for her child.

Something else happens to many women right after the birth of her first baby. A woman may start to have fleeting sensations of what it was like to be a baby herself. Memories of her own childhood come rushing back to her, including odd sensory experiences, such as how it felt to stroke her mother's dress or breathe her scent, to be empty and cold, to be gently sung to. These memories enable a woman to feel empathy for her baby, but they may also cause her to long to be looked after in a loving way. She may ache to be nurtured and there may be no one who realizes how great her need is. So it is not surprising that she grieves the loss of her own infancy and childhood.

Sometimes her memories may cause her to remember—perhaps for the first time—that she was neglected or abused, so she may grieve for the childhood she was cheated of.

When a woman has had a job and is now at home with her baby, either because she is on maternity leave or because she is not returning to work, she may grieve the loss of mobility, independence, and the satisfaction and self-esteem she achieved from her job.

DEPRESSION

Women in particular undergo tremendous changes in their lives when they have a baby, especially the birth of a first baby. Many women feel they have lost their identity as they struggle to come to terms with the challenges of motherhood. But there is more to it than that. Postnatal depression is frequently the result of being treated as a patient, incapable of knowing how to care for her baby at a time when she is taking on the responsibility of a new life and needs to assess information, weigh alternatives, and come to important decisions. Those close to her may tell her she is worrying too much, criticize her for letting her baby rule her life, accuse her of being overemotional, of talking too much about a distressing birth when she ought to "forget" it, or of being obsessional about wanting to breast-feed. All this well-meaning advice and criticism may cause a woman to feel misunderstood, angry, and out of control, which can in turn lead to depression.

MEN'S EMOTIONAL CHANGES

In the early stages of pregnancy, men are apt to undergo periods of self-doubt, in part because so much is expected of them. Many worry about whether they will be able to meet the expectations of their partner, of their child, and of society in general. But because men typically do not give themselves permission to acknowledge and express their emotions, many deny their fears. Unfortunately, this often causes them to shut down altogether, giving them the appearance of not caring enough, being too laid-back or even of being apathetic. This is due to the fact that once we begin distancing ourselves from our emotions, we find that *all* our feelings become muted or even deadened.

Nine months of pregnancy leaves a great deal of time for thinking, anticipating, and worrying for both parents, but expectant mothers usually have other women to talk to about their concerns and feel more free to talk to their partners about them. Men, on the other hand, often keep their concerns to themselves. Because their partners talk to them so often about their fears, men often feel they must be the strong ones.

Men begin to worry from the time they first hear the news but most especially when they feel the baby move for the first time, bringing home the tangible reality of a growing fetus. They worry over whether their partner is getting enough rest, adequate exercise, and good nutrition. They worry if there are complications, such as long-term morning sickness, bleeding, or pain. As the estimated date of arrival nears, a myriad of questions often arise: "Will the labor be difficult?" "How can I be most helpful?" "Will I be helpful enough?" "Will I be able to handle watching the birth, seeing the blood and seeing my partner in pain?" "Do I want to cut the cord?" "Will our baby be born healthy?" "What if he or she isn't? Will I be able to handle it?"

Fortunately, the nine months of pregnancy also provides time to take stock, integrate the subtle changes, and prepare for the reality of becoming a parent. Some men manage to adjust to their new identity by midpregnancy. Others remain uneasy until their baby is born—or sometime afterward. Still others never overcome their discomfort and, unfortunately, retreat from fatherhood altogether.

Men too often sense an undercurrent of loss prior to and following the birth of a child. In addition to feeling left out and unable to involve himself to any meaningful degree in the pregnancy, an expectant father may miss the exclusivity of his prepregnancy relationship with his partner. He may begin to experience feelings of frustration, jealousy, and insecurity, es-

pecially if his needs are continually overshadowed by his partner's. These feelings are often hard for men to accept, since
they are taught that displays of jealousy and insecurity expose
them as weak and unmasculine and that feelings of frustration
are to be handled and controlled, rather than discussed (which
is viewed as complaining or, worse yet, whining).

Many men try to escape from their feelings of hurt, discomfort, frustration, or fear by withdrawing—investing themselves in work, hobbies, or relationships outside the family.
While taking time for themselves can sometimes renew their
enthusiasm and provide a different perspective, running from
uncomfortable situations can become an habitual escape.

Often the emotions that are stirred up in response to
pregnancy and childbirth are reminders of childhood pain and
catapult men back into memories of neglect, invalidation, criticism, or lack of love. These unhealed emotional wounds can
cause men to attempt to numb their pain with alcohol or drugs
or to lash out in anger. These actions will, of course, further
undermine their efforts to solidify their relationship with their
partner.

If potential fathers are willing to allow themselves to fully
experience all their emotions, even the so-called "negative"
ones, such as their fear, guilt, and anger, they will find that
they are also able to feel more joy, pride, satisfaction, and
eager anticipation about their new role of father.

Many fathers, once the baby is born, experience an unpar-
alleled emotional high, a surge of pride and self-esteem. Along
with this high can come a new surge of apprehension. Many
men have difficulty relating to a new baby, requiring substantial amounts of time and interaction before comfort and ease
set in. Some become impatient, looking for their child to smile
or show some sign of interest or some glimmer of recognition.
Others prefer to step back and observe more experienced caretakers or look to their partners for the guidance and validation

needed to gain confidence in themselves as fathers. Again, none of these reactions should be considered "wrong." The important thing is to stay in touch with your primary emotions and find a parenting style that is comfortable for you and for your partner.

Physical Changes

A woman's body definitely goes through some rather dramatic physical changes as the result of pregnancy and birth. Some of the changes she will experience include:

- The shape of her vagina is different.
- She may not feel the degree of sexual arousal that she did before.
- It may be difficult to lose weight gained in pregnancy.
- Pregnancy can cause varicose veins and stretch marks.

After childbirth, the area between a woman's vagina and her anus—the perineum—is often sore, bruised, and tender. Many women endure a knob of aching, prickly scar tissue below the vagina because they have had an episiotomy that had to be sewn up afterward. This is uncomfortable when sitting, throbs when she is standing, and may make sexual intercourse so painful that penetration is impossible for several months. This can cause self-consciousness and strain in a couple's relationship. Although many women say, "My husband is so understanding," it can lead to sexual problems and conflict in a relationship, and almost invariably women believe that it is somehow their "fault."

Some women feel sexually recharged and long to make love within days of giving birth. Others find it takes much longer than this to be fully aroused—sometimes so long that they become anxious that they will never be able to re-create a happy and spontaneous sexual relationship. Being sleep-deprived also contributes to a new mother's lack of sexual interest. Even when a baby begins to sleep through the night, many mothers find that all their energy, creative imagination, and emotions may be focused on mothering for most of the first year after birth.

Many women are anxious about or afraid of intercourse because they are in pain, they are weak and worn out, or they hate how their bodies look and feel after having a baby. It is as if they have been unsexed. Following a cesarean birth, abdominal tenderness may make a woman shrink from any vigorous lovemaking, whether or not it involves genital sex, because she feels so vulnerable.

With all this happening, it is not uncommon for women to feel at times as if a hoax has been played on them. "Why didn't anyone warn them about these things," they may ask themselves. "If I'd have known I was going to go through all this, I'd never had this baby," they may think in silence. Indeed, women do need to be prepared for all the above possibilities and they should keep them in mind as they make their decision as to whether or not to have a baby.

Commitment

Becoming a good parent, not just a parent, involves a total and lasting commitment on your part. This means you must have a "burning desire" to be the best parent you can possibly be, just as you would bring to any other major life decision.

Some people fear that they don't have the level of commitment necessary to become good parents. This was the case with Zena:

"My parents were totally involved with us kids, which makes me appreciate that to do it right requires incredible dedication. I'm not sure I have that kind of commitment. It would mean so much time and self-sacrifice, leaving little time for anything else. My mother sacrificed her career as a dancer to stay home with us kids and make sure we were happy. And I know my dad could have gone much further in his career if he hadn't spent so much time coaching the boys in Little League and attending my dance recitals. I have a career that I love and I'm not sure I'm willing to sacrifice it for a child."

Still others are unsure they can make a lifelong commitment to a child because they have problems with commitments in general, as Gracie told me when she came in for therapy:

"Let's face it. I don't do commitments well. Even though I've been with Mitch for four years now, this is the longest relationship I've been in. I didn't intend to get pregnant, it just happened. Mitch wants to be a father and I know he'd be a good one, but I'm not so sure I have what it takes to be a good parent. The whole idea scares me. Sometimes I think it would be best for the child and for me if I put the baby up for adoption. I'm just not sure."

Still others value personal freedom so much they doubt that they would be willing to tolerate the restrictions that children impose. These people need to feel unconfined emotionally as well as physically in order to have the spontaneity they need and treasure, as was the case with Lucy:

"I'm basically what they call a 'free spirit.' I love being able to pick up and do what I want, to decide at the spur of the moment what I want to do next without feeling guilt or worrying about logistics. I'm afraid a child is going to tie me down too much, that I'll feel too confined."

The following exercise will help you project into the future and test your level of commitment to being a good parent.

EXERCISE: Testing Your Commitment

- Imagine this scenario: You've finally saved enough money for you and your mate to go on a cruise. It's the first vacation you've had together since you had your first child, ten years ago. You are just about to go to the travel agency at lunchtime when your wife calls to tell you that your oldest daughter, Heather, needs braces. "Thank God we have that money socked away," she says. "Otherwise, I don't know what we'd do. Our dental insurance doesn't pay for braces."

How do you imagine you'd feel? Resentful? Probably. Angry? Maybe. Grateful that you do, in fact, have the money? Probably not, at least not at the moment. While it would be natural for you to feel angry and resentful for a time, your parental feelings of love and commitment toward your child should eventually take over, causing you to let go of these emotions and gladly spend the money on your child's health.

• Here's another scenario to imagine: You and your husband have just bought a new car. The first new car you've ever had. You've given your old car to your teenage son with strict instructions that he cannot drive the new car *under any circumstances*. Late one night, the phone rings. It's the police. Your son has been in an accident. He's all right, but he's been arrested for drunk driving. Horrified, you and your husband get out of bed, get dressed, and rush down to the car to go pick him up at the police station. As you open the garage door, you are shocked again. Instead of seeing your shiny new car sitting in the garage, you see only your son's car.

After you bail your son out of jail, you go to the police impound station to pick up your new car. It's totaled. What's more, your son has been excluded on your auto insurance policy from driving the new car, so you aren't sure they'll pay to get you a new one. And even if they do, you're certain they won't replace your car with a brand-new one.

How do you imagine you'd feel? Again, probably furious and rightly so. Do you think you'd get over it eventually and forgive your son or continue to resent him for a long time afterward?

Becoming a parent requires the ability to not only put your own needs aside for the welfare of your child but to be able to love your child *unconditionally* and to forgive your child his or her faults, weaknesses, and even major blunders.

In addition to being willing to cope with all that parenting entails, being a parent also means a willingness on your part to change those things about your environment, personality, and your relationship that will get in the way of you providing your child with the love, security, and stability every child needs.

This may mean being willing to move to a new area where the schools are better and there is less crime, even though it will mean a commute to you. It may mean being willing to stop drinking or taking drugs. It may mean seeking marriage counseling to help you resolve conflicts in your relationship. Part IV will elaborate more on what it takes to be a good parent, which will, in turn, help you to further determine your willingness to be a parent.

It may seem that outlining the changes you will go through as new parents is painting a grim picture of parenthood. But it is important that you be prepared for the inevitable changes you will go through.

Although many of the changes new parents go through may seem to be negative, by being prepared and by facing the challenges these changes create, these negatives can be turned into positives. Deciding to have a baby will definitely be challenging but challenges can stimulate constructive change. Parenthood can be a time of personal growth in which you learn a lot about yourself, your relationship, develop new skills, and discover what you are made of.

And although reading about parenthood can educate you

and give you an idea of what to expect, nothing can prepare you for the positive emotions that a baby can bring. In spite of the fact that there will be times when you lose all self-confidence and feel that you are a terrible parent, there will be other times when you feel a wonderful contentment. And no one can question the fact that having a child is one of the most joyous experiences one can experience in life.

Part IV

Are You Able to Be

a Good Parent?

NINE

Taking a Close Look at Yourself
as a Potential Parent

DETERMINING whether you are able to be a good parent may be the most difficult issue for potential parents to tackle. As I stated earlier, not every person who *wants* to have children *should* have children. And no matter how much you feel you are ready for parenthood, nearly every potential parent has some concerns or fears about whether they have what it takes to be a *good* parent.

Some people are concerned that they do not have the personality to be a good parent. They may already be aware of certain shortcomings or personal problems that they fear might get in their way of being good parents, such as a lack of patience, a tendency to be somewhat selfish or preoccupied, a tendency to be overly critical, or a problem with their anger.

Others are concerned because they themselves did not have parents who possessed the qualities, nor the parenting skills necessary for good parenting. Realizing the handicaps they have had to overcome, these potential parents are concerned they may make the same mistakes as their parents. For example, this is what my client Katie told me about her concerns:

"My mother was incredibly selfish. Instead of thinking of my needs, she almost always put her own first. This included the food she bought, the movies we saw, even the clothes and toys she bought me. I'm so afraid I'll end up like her or that I'll overcompensate by going overboard and spoiling my kids."

For some, these fears are based on the awareness that they had abusive, neglectful, or absent parents. Fearful that they will repeat the pattern of abuse or neglect with their own children, they hesitate about becoming a parent. Some are afraid they will repeat the cycle of emotional, physical, or sexual abuse that has been passed down in their families for generations. This was the case with Derek, another client of mine:

"My dad beat me because his dad beat him, and there's even some evidence that my grandfather's dad beat *him*. I don't want to pass on this family legacy, but I have a bad temper and I know how these things work. My wife wants a child very badly, but I'm afraid to take the chance. How can I be sure I won't end up doing the same things that were done to me?"

In this chapter, I will help you take a close look at yourself as a potential parent. While this self-examination may seem tedious and can be painful, it will do more than almost anything else to ally your fears and concerns about whether you will be a good parent. It will also uncover those areas you need to work on in order to better prepare yourself for parenthood.

In addition, by presenting the most common concerns potential parents have about their ability to be good parents and by sharing some case examples of previous clients, my hope is that I will help you discover you are not alone with your apprehensions and will therefore encourage you to be more willing to take a close look at your own issues.

Taking a Look at Your Personality

In this section, I will help you take a good hard look at the kind of personality you have and whether it is conducive to parenting. I will ask questions and provide information that will help you explore such areas as:

- how patient or impatient you are
- how you handle your emotions
- how you handle stress
- how disciplined and consistent you are
- your ability to bond emotionally with others
- your level of self-esteem

Questions: Taking a Close Look at Your Personality

We'll start by having you answer the following questions. These are intended to help you begin to focus on issues that are important to parenting. Take your time and be as honest as possible. The process of answering the questions is as important as the answers themselves.

1. Are you a patient person? What is your tolerance for noise and confusion? Are you patient with children?

2. Do you enjoy teaching others? Do you enjoy explaining things to others? Are you patient if someone doesn't seem to be learning as quickly or easily as you'd like?

3. How flexible are you? Is it important to you to do what you want when you want or are you willing to compromise and delay gratification? How do you imagine your family and friends would rate your flexibility?

4. Do you anger easily? If so, what actions have you

taken to learn to handle your anger more constructively? What kinds of behaviors and events anger you the most? Would friends or family describe you as an angry person?

5. How does it make you feel to be out of control? Is feeling out of control or helpless a frightening feeling to you? How do you react when you cannot control a situation? Do you feel there is a right way to do things? How important is it for you to be right?

6. Do you tend to be judgmental or critical? Do you find fault easily?

7. How important do you feel discipline is in raising a child? If your child does not obey you, how will you handle it? Do you feel competent to set up rules and enforce them? Do you tend to be consistent in your behavior and viewpoints? How important will it be for you to be popular and well-liked by your child?

8. How important is personal freedom to you? How much of your personal freedom are you willing to give up in order to be responsible for a child?

Again, there are no right or wrong answers to the above questions. They are intended to help you take an honest, objective look at your personality in regards to parenthood.

Do You Have the Personality to Be a Good Parent?

Although there isn't a "parent" personality, there are certain personality characteristics that predispose one to parenting, certain traits that most good parents have in common. These traits are:

- patience
- flexibility
- tolerance for intrusion

- the ability to put oneself aside for prolonged periods of time without experiencing deep resentment or anger

Patience

The truth is, some of us are more patient than others. Those who are patient don't mind waiting in a grocery checkout line or getting stuck on the freeway quite as much as those who are impatient. It's not that these people don't feel inconvenienced or even frustrated. It's just that they are able to take it in stride more than those who tend to be impatient. They are able to relax into the moment more than their restless counterparts, to utilize the delay to get their thoughts together, make plans, or just daydream.

An impatient person, on the other hand, has little tolerance for waiting. They tend to be goal-oriented and some tend to be a bit controlling, resenting anything that gets in the way of achieving their goals. Instead of begrudgingly accepting a delay, their tension increases every minute they have to wait.

Parenting requires patience. Children do things slowly. They dawdle and daydream and do things the wrong way. They make messes that take time to clean up. They seem to have the uncanny ability to create a delay of some kind whenever their parents are in a hurry.

It is impatient, goal-oriented parents who tend to become the most frustrated with their children. This frustration can, in turn, cause parents to become controlling or even abusive.

The following scenario is a good example of how a parent's impatience can lead to controlling, demeaning, and frightening behavior:

Geneva is bent on getting to the department store when the doors open in order to take advantage of a fantastic white sale. She got up extra-early, allowing herself plenty of time to get her five-year-old son David dressed and fed before getting dressed herself. As she's finishing getting dressed, she calls to David to get his coat on and to meet her at the front door. Glancing at the clock, she assures herself she has plenty of time, takes a deep breath, and walks downstairs. Expecting to see David at the door, she impatiently calls upstairs for him. There is no answer. She puts down her purse and huffs up the stairs to find him. When she walks into his room, she finds David in his underwear, quietly and calmly sorting through his dresser drawers.

"What are you doing? Why are you undressed?" she asks, her voice going up an octave or two.

"I want to wear my red shirt."

"Fine," she says, pushing him aside in her haste to find the shirt. "But why did you have to take off your pants? Put them back on this instant."

A dejected David slowly starts to put on his pants while Geneva jerks open another drawer, scattering clothes in her desperate search for David's red shirt. Realizing that her son can be stubborn (no doubt in response to his mother's controlling behavior), Geneva knows better than to try to talk him out of wearing his favorite shirt. Finally, she finds it at the bottom of a drawer.

"Here, here it is. Now put it on!" she commands as she turns to find David sitting on the edge of his bed, one leg in a pant leg, the other out.

"My God, David, hurry up. What's taking you so long?"

"I don't like these pants."

"What do you mean? We just bought those pants."

"I don't want to wear them today."

Totally exasperated, Geneva looks at her watch. "We don't have time for this today, David. Come on. Get those pants on right now."

Glancing up at his mother, David decides not to push his mother today. He can tell by the tone of her voice that it would be a mistake. Ever so slowly, he begins to slide his leg into his pant leg.

Geneva swoops over to him, stuffs him into his pants, and snaps them around his waist. "Now come on!" she says as she pulls him down the stairs and pushes him out the door.

As you can imagine, Geneva and David are in for a stressful day. David, resenting the fact that his mother is rushing him and pushing him around, will eventually have a major temper tantrum in the department store. Geneva will have to cut her shopping trip short to save herself from the embarrassment of others watching as her son thrashes around on the floor, screaming at the top of his lungs.

Had she been a more patient person, she would have taken the shirt and pants incident in stride, tried to understand her son's need to change clothes, and quietly helped him to do so. Since she's allowed herself enough time, she would have realized the few minutes' delay wasn't going to make that much of a difference. And she would have been able to remind herself that, after all, her son was far more important than getting to the store early for the sale. Consequently, she would have saved herself a lot of hassle and had a far more pleasant day.

The point here is that children are unpredictable, often stubborn, often difficult, and hardly ever cooperative when it comes to a timetable. To try to force them into a schedule without recognizing that there will be inevitable delays is only inviting frustration. While some parents learn this lesson and eventually learn to be patient, most who are impatient never learn it or learn it the hard way—after they have become dictatorial or abusive to their children.

Flexibility

In addition to patience, parents need to be flexible. It simply isn't possible for parents to plan or exert the same control over their lives once they have a child. Learning and practicing flexibility simply makes life easier.

Flexible people have an easier time choosing which battles are worth fighting and which are not. This goes a long way in parenting. For example, in the previous example, had Geneva been a bit more flexible, she could have saved herself and her son a lot of grief. A more flexible parent would have taken a deep breath when she found her son undressed and let go of her insistence on getting to the store as the doors opened. Parents who are flexible find it easier to give their children choices in regard to small things, which then makes it easier for them to accept unilateral decisions when they occur. Overall, this makes for greater parent/child cooperation.

And, of course, raising a child is always an unpredictable project in the long run, and this presents difficulties for people who like to be in charge. You just can't write the script for your child's life and guarantee the outcome; you must have the flexibility to accept what children ultimately choose to do—and not do—with their futures. Any other course of action is a way to heartbreak for you and your child.

Tolerance for Intrusion

Becoming a parent also means giving up your physical and emotional space. Children are by nature intrusive, climbing all over you, interrupting your conversations and your work, insisting on your attention. And the greatest intrusion of all, the noise that children inevitably and quite naturally make, epitomizes the feeling of being intruded upon. The decibel level of life automatically rises around even the best-behaved child. Parents must learn to endure a cacophony of sound ranging from ear-piercing crying and yelling to the irritating beeps and crashes of video games and the repetitious singing of *Sesame Street* songs.

For some, the idea of sharing their physical and emotional

space with a child on a full-time basis creates a feeling of claus-trophobia. The truth is, some people have temperaments and histories that make them sensitive to intrusion. If you are one of the many people who require privacy and uninterrupted time for your well-being, the mere idea of parenting may be stressful for you, as it was with my client, Rebecca:

"I know I wouldn't do well as a parent. I'd get too frazzled. I need long stretches of time alone in order to maintain my equilibrium and keep from being overstimulated and exhausted by the pace of life in Los Angeles—the freeway congestion and the sounds of ambulances, car alarms, and rap music blasting out of cars."

One of the major stressors for some parents is the fact that they feel so intruded upon emotionally by their children. They feel as if they no longer have a life separate from their child, that because children can be so emotionally demanding, they no longer have the emotional reserves for self-reflection, much less for their partner. This was the case with Emily, who entered therapy when her oldest child was ten years old:

"I feel emotionally smothered by my children. They demand so much of my attention and the intimacy is so intense between us that I feel I am being robbed of my individuality. I seldom have any time to myself. Instead, it all seems to be racing by with little consciousness on my part. Each day is like the next. I've stopped growing. I'm the kids' parent and any other time and energy I have left is devoted to being a wife. I've lost who I was before I had kids and I want to get it back."

Some, either because of their temperament or their history, find a child's constant, unavoidable presence and chronic need for attention burdensome. This was the case with my client Clare:

"A child is always right there. You can't ignore its needs. Mothers don't even have one or two hours a day to themselves. You're expected to put yourself on hold, put all your own needs aside. I just don't know if I can do that. I'm afraid I'd grow to resent my child or, worse, to hate him or her for taking all my time."

The Ability to Put Oneself Aside

Parenthood requires sacrifices both great and small. On a daily basis, parents must put their own needs and desires aside for the sake of their children. Starting when their baby is first born and even before, parents must put aside their need for sleep, for sex with their partner, and for pursuing interests and activities outside the home. Some people are able to make meeting their child's needs their top priority and are happy to do it. For these people, gratification far outweighs any feelings of frustration, deprivation, anger, or resentment.

Others, however, have problems with such extreme self-sacrifice, either because it echoes times in their lives when they sacrificed themselves to their own detriment or because it reminds them of their own parents' sacrifices.

Women who feel they have never been able to be their own person can experience children as an infringement and conclude they are not right for the job. This was the case with Helene, a woman I interviewed for the book:

"My parents wanted me to become a nurse, so I gave up my desire to become an artist. Then I sacrificed my college education so that my first husband could finish school. I'm through sacrificing."

And still others cannot put their own needs aside to raise a child simply because their own needs are too great. Some were so deprived or neglected as children that they find it difficult to respond to other people's needs, as was the situation with Consuela:

"I have too many unmet needs of my own to even attempt to meet the needs of a child. I still long to be nurtured and held myself, I'm still looking for a mother."

If you do not have the above-listed qualities, it doesn't mean there is anything wrong with you or that you are deficient in some way. The most important thing is that you are able to see yourself clearly. At that point, you can make an informed decision about whether you want to work toward changing these things about yourself or are content to leave things as they are. Ultimately, you may discover you aren't as suited to parenthood as someone else, just as you may not be as suited to a particular profession.

EXERCISE: What Is a Good Parent?

- Make a list of the traits you feel are necessary for good parenting.
- Now take a good look at your list. Do you feel you have some or most of these qualities? Or do you recognize that you lack many of these qualities?

The following is my own list of the most desirable characteristics for parents.

A good parent is able:

- to emotionally bond with their child
- to be patient and tolerant with their child
- to handle stress in a positive way
- to put their needs and problems temporarily aside in order to meet the needs of their child
- to find adequate outlets for their negative emotions
- to find ways to get their needs met by adults instead of expecting their child to meet them
- to have reasonable expectations of their child
- to love their child unconditionally (to dislike their behavior but love the child)
- to devote a great deal of their time and energy to taking care

of their child's needs without taking their anger out on their child or inducing guilt in their child
- to feel protective of their child
- to allow their child the space and encouragement to grow into their own unique person

While you will most likely compare your list with mine, it is as important for you to feel you will be a good parent based on your *own* list of characteristics as it is for you to meet the qualifications of experts such as myself. If you meet the criteria of the so-called experts but do not meet your own, you will likely be overly critical of yourself and remain dissatisfied with yourself as a parent. This, in turn, will affect your children.

Both of these lists will be a starting-off point for further discussion. For example, in the upcoming chapter specifically for those in a relationship, I will ask you to have your partner make his or her own list of the traits of a good parent and then to compare your lists.

Your Attitude Toward Children

Another important factor determining whether you have what it takes to be a good parent is your attitude toward children. Again, although there isn't a "right" or "wrong" attitude to have toward children, there are certain attitudes that are more constructive and child-positive.

While it may seem obvious that those who choose to be parents enjoy and like children, this is not always true. Genuinely liking children is different from loving your sister's child or the fantasies you have about how much you will love your own. It involves being sincerely interested in children, what they have to say, and how they act. It means you enjoy their company, enjoy their activities, and enjoy playing with them.

Many people, even those who want a child very badly, do not actually like children. They find them uninteresting or even boring, as is the case with Dena:

"I can take kids for just so long and then I get bored. I mean, you can't really carry on a conversation with them. After you say, 'Hello, how are you?', 'What's your name?', 'What grade are you in?', 'What's your favorite subject?', and 'What do you want to be when you grow up?'—what else is there to talk about? I've always assumed this won't be the case when I have my own kids, but sometimes I wonder."

Others are uncomfortable or even threatened by children. This is how Robert explained it to me:

"I'm always uneasy around children. It's crazy because, after all, I'm the adult. But I actually feel a little intimidated by them. I'm always afraid they won't like me and I keep expecting them to say some hurtful, cruel comment to me the way kids do. I think it's because I was mercilessly teased by other kids when I was growing up."

Neither Dena nor Robert should assume that they will feel any more comfortable around their own children than they feel around others'. While Dena would certainly have more of an investment in her own children and be more concerned about their welfare, she lacks the ability to relate to children, to identify with them. And while Robert would no doubt be more comfortable with his own children, just because they will be more familiar to him, this will not necessarily alleviate the problem of him feeling intimidated by them.

I encourage you to take some time exploring your attitudes toward children. The following questions will help you do so.

Questions: Your Attitude Toward Children

1. Have you spent a lot of time around babies or small children?

2. Are you comfortable around children? Or do you become bored? Intimidated?

3. Do you like children? Do you enjoy being around them? What are the specific things you like the most? What do you like the least?

4. Do you enjoy playing with children? Do you like the activities that interest them?

5. When it is time to leave their presence, do you generally feel more sorry or more relieved?

If you recognize through these questions and some soul-searching that you do not have the kind of personality or attitudes toward children that are most conducive to parenting, take heart. This does not mean that you *shouldn't* become a parent as much as it means you have some work to do on yourself and that perhaps you need to wait before becoming a parent. While our personality is set by the time we reach adulthood, this does not mean you cannot work toward changing certain aspects of your personality, such as patience and flexibility.

On the other hand, answering these questions may have validated the feelings you've had along. For example, you may have already suspected that you would have a difficult time putting your needs aside to devote your time to a child. This is what Leslie told me after answering the questions I posed:

"I always suspected that perhaps I wasn't 'mother material.' When my best friend Clarissa had her baby, I noticed that I only wanted to hold it for a little while and then I got very uncomfortable. She assured me it was because the baby wasn't my own, but I suspected it was more than that. I started to feel trapped sitting there with the baby and I imagined how it would feel if I had to hold it all the time—you know, to feed it and comfort it. It kind of turned me off, the idea that someone was so dependent on me. Then when I read those questions and really thought about it, I realized I didn't have what it takes to be a good parent. In a way, I feel relieved because everyone is always trying to talk me into being a mother. I should have trusted my gut instincts all along, but I guess I just didn't have the courage to stand up to them all. Now I feel more secure about my decision, like I have something substantial to back me up."

Your personality, including your ability to be patient and flexible, to handle intrusion, and to put oneself aside, is partly determined by your upbringing and the experiences you had as a child. The same is true for your attitudes toward children. The following chapter will help you to focus on the messages you received from your upbringing, including your parents' attitude toward children in general and their attitude toward you in particular.

TEN

Taking a Close Look at Your Childhood and Your Family History

FEW THINGS affect the shaping of your personality and your ability to be a good parent more than your own childhood experiences and your family history. The information in this chapter will help you to make the all important connection between your past and your present. In addition, it will provide you with relevant information about yourself that will help you to make the kind of changes in yourself that can make the difference between being an inadequate parent and being a good one.

EXERCISE: Your Parents' Attitude Toward Children

1. Think about your own parents in relationship to what you've just read about the type of personality bestsuited for parenting. Did your parents exhibit the qualities of patience, flexibility, tolerance for intrusion, and the ability to put oneself

aside? How do you imagine your parents would answer the questions I posed?

2. Now think about the attitudes your parents had toward children: you, in particular. Did you get the feeling as you were growing up that your parents really liked you, liked spending time with you, playing with you? Did they seem genuinely interested in your activities and interests? Or did they give the impression that you were in the way or that they were just tolerating you?

Parental attitudes toward children are very powerful and it is likely that you have taken on many of the same ways of thinking about children as your parents. Notice how your parents refer to children and their attitudes toward them now. Then compare your own attitudes with theirs.

Taking a Look at Your Own Childhood

Probably the most significant factors determining your capacity to be a good parent are: whether or not you had a healthy bonding experience with your own parents, how you were treated by your parents as you were growing up, the kind of family life you experienced, and whether you were emotionally, physically, or sexually abused as a child or adolescent. We will explore all these issues in the following section.

Bonding

One of the major requirements for being a good parent is the capacity to love and share intimacy with another human being. We gain this capacity primarily by experiencing a healthy bonding experience with our parents—most particularly, our mothers. In fact, the relationship between infant and mother is the single most important factor contributing to the emotional as well as physical health of the child. It is through our mother's loving touch that we are given the ability to love ourselves and to love others.

Research shows that the amount and kind of touching we received as infants and young children strongly affects both our ability to become intimate with another person and our urge to nurture. For the human being to learn to give love, he or she must first receive love.

When a child is provided with enough nurturing and safety, he or she is taught that intimacy and personal involvement are not to be feared and that opening up psychologically to a significant other is nurturing instead of dangerous. On the other hand, the child who is pushed away, neglected, or smothered by his or her parents' love learns that intimate contact is too risky and may grow up preferring alienation or empty relationships to the vulnerability of genuine intimacy.

While it is difficult to determine whether or not you received adequate touching and nurturing as an infant and small child, most of us have an internal sense as to how much touching we received. In addition to this internal sense, you can begin to put the pieces of the puzzle together by answering the following questions:

Questions: Your Capacity for Loving

1. Are your parents affectionate with you now?
2. Are you a demonstrative person? Are you affectionate? Do you like to touch and be touched?
3. Is it easy for you to express your feelings of love and affection or is it difficult? If it is difficult, why do you think this is so?
4. Is loving someone easy or difficult for you? If difficult, why do you think this is true?
5. What is your history with intimate relationships?

6. Do you often feel stiff, uncomfortable, or smothered by someone else's affection or other expressions of love?

The Way You Were Treated as a Child

We tend to treat our children the way our parents treated us. If you grew up in a loving, relatively healthy household, then this is good news. It means that more than likely, the time, attention, support, and love you received from your parents gave you the necessary foundation that every child needs in order to grow into a healthy adult. It means that your parents were positive role models who inadvertently taught you how to be a good parent by their actions, beliefs, and attitudes. If your family life was mostly a positive one, filled with happy memories and security, you have been blessed with a positive image of family and childhood and this will no doubt carry over when you begin your own family.

On the other hand, if your childhood was fraught with unhappiness, neglect, chaos, tragedy, or abuse, the news is not so good. If you grew up around alcoholic parents, parents who continually fought, parents who were often unavailable to you, or parents who were physically, sexually, or emotionally abusive to you or your siblings, you are probably already aware of the damage you suffered and the effects that this behavior has had on your life. What you may not be aware of is specifically how these experiences affect your ability to be a good parent.

Some of you may not be too certain what kind of a childhood you really had. You may not have many clear memories of your childhood or you may not be sure whether certain behaviors were, in fact, abusive. For this reason, it is very important to take a good look at your home life in order to get a clear picture of exactly what your childhood was like and in order to assess the damage you may have experienced.

Questions: Your Home Life

1. How would you describe your household as you were growing up? Mostly peaceful? Often chaotic? Depressing? Frightening?

2. How did your parents treat you most of the time? Were they loving and kind or harsh and critical?

3. Were your parents cold or detached? Overbearing, domineering? Neglectful?

4. Was one or both of your parents overly attached or overprotective of you?

5. Did one or both of your parents favor one of your siblings over another?

6. Were either of your parents physically abusive to you?

7. Did anyone in your family—father, mother, sibling, grandparent—touch you in an inappropriately sexual way?

8. Do you think that you will treat your children the same way you were treated by members of your family?

9. Do you think you will parent in the opposite way?

10. What measures have you taken to ensure you will not be like your parents?

11. If you were abused, in what ways can you be sure you will not inflict abuse on your own children?

12. How is your relationship with your own parents today? Do you have a warm, loving relationship or is there constant tension between you? Do you avoid seeing one or both of your parents? If so, for what reason? If one or both of your parents are dead, do you remember them with primarily positive or negative feelings?

13. Would you be comfortable having one or both of your parents baby-sit for your children? If not, why is that? Are there attitudes or behaviors that your parents display that you strongly disagree with and would like to shield your children from? If so, what are these, specifically?

14. Are there aspects of your personality that you recognize as being very much like one or both of your parents? Are these aspects positive or negative? What aspects would you like to pass along to your children? Which would you like to avoid bringing to a child?

Looking closely at your childhood can bring forth a multitude of emotions: gratitude, distress, joy, and anger have undoubtedly all been provoked in you as you considered your family legacy.

While many people have happy childhoods and positive memories of the parenting they received, many others know that their childhood was marked by a great deal of turbulence and inconsistency. In the next few pages, I will outline some of the more negative parenting patterns some children experience.

Recognizing Abuse

In looking closely at your childhood, some of you may not be certain whether the environment you grew up in was healthy or not or whether or not you were abused as a child. The following information will help clarify this for you.

Physical Abuse

Physical abuse is any physical show of force for the purposes of intimidating, threatening, or controlling another person. Physical abuse includes slapping, hitting, punching, kicking, pushing, tripping, burning, biting, or pinching whenever it is done in anger. Other acts of physical abuse include throwing objects at the person, using an object to hit a person, holding someone down, forcing someone to sit or lie in a certain position, forcing someone's arms behind their back, and pinning someone down. Face-slapping, hair-pulling, head-banging, ear-pulling, or shaking can also be abusive.

Sexual Abuse

Sexual abuse is any exploitation of a child for the sexual gratification of an adult or an older child. It includes exhibitionism (exposing oneself to a child), voyeurism (becoming sexually aroused by surreptitiously watching a child undress, bathe, or use the toilet), fondling, digital penetration or penetrating the child using inanimate objects, intercourse, or using the child to produce pornographic materials.

Many forms of sexual abuse do not involve intercourse or any kind of penetration. Of equal importance is any indirect or direct sexual suggestion made by an adult toward a child. This is called "approach behavior." It can include sexual looks, innuendoes, or suggestive gestures. Even if the adult never engages in touching or takes any overt sexual action, the child picks up these projected sexual feelings.

If you have any questions about what constitutes childhood sexual abuse, please refer to Appendix II for recommended books that will further clarify this for you.

Emotional Incest

Emotional incest can be defined as a parent becoming overly involved and overly invested in his or her child's life. This may take the form of being overly possessive and not wanting her child to have friends or to begin dating. It may take the form of making the child into a sort of "surrogate mate" by treating the child like a lover or spouse. Or it may take the form of seductiveness and intrusion.

Many parents walk a fine line between emotional and sexual incest. Even though these parents may never touch their children inappropriately, they display an unhealthy interest in their child's body by either openly staring at their bodies, by taking seductive pictures of them, by making inappropriate sexual remarks, or by not allowing their children privacy in the bedroom or bathroom.

Two of the many effects of emotional incest are chronic relationship problems and a curious blend of high and low self-esteem:

When Janette was growing up, she and her father acted more like a happily married couple than father and daughter. They went everywhere together, leaving her mother at home with her little brother. She was the one who attended social functions with her father, whether it was a company dance or the movies on Saturday night.

When boys began to notice Janette, her father acted more like a jealous boyfriend than a father. He refused to let her date until she was eighteen and then he was critical of each boy she went out with. Janette began to lie to her father and sneak out on dates with men, many of whom were either married or involved with drugs, gambling, or crime.

"I know now that I was just acting out against my father's possessiveness. I needed some space from him and somehow these kind of men, who were as different from my father as could possibly be, provided me with that sense of space. Unfortunately, my self-esteem was further damaged because I felt so guilty going against my father and because the men I got involved with usually ended up either using me or dumping me."

Sexual problems are common among victims of emotional incest. Because the child and adult are in essence more like intimate partners than family members, it is natural for sexual feelings to arise. This sexual energy then must be dealt with, either expressed or repressed. The child may choose to express the sexuality in the form of excessive masturbation or promiscuity or repress their sexuality and later pay the price of sexual dysfunction or lack of sexual desire. This is especially true if there are rigid and strict family injunctions against sex.

Emotional Abuse

Emotional abuse is any kind of abuse that is emotional rather than physical in nature. It can include anything from verbal abuse and constant criticism to more subtle tactics, such as intimidation, manipulation, and refusal to ever be pleased.

Emotional abuse is like brainwashing in that it systematically wears away at the victim's self-confidence, sense of self-worth, trust in his or her perceptions, and self-concept. Whether it is done by constant berating and belittling, by intimidation, or under the guise of "guidance" or "teaching," the results are similar. Eventually, the recipient of the abuse loses a sense of self and personal value.

Children of alcoholics are emotionally abused in a number of ways, most notably by being neglected physically and emotionally, abandoned, by being verbally abused, by having to take on responsibilities before they are mature enough to do so, and by suffering unpredictability and a chaotic home environment.

Many people are not aware that they were emotionally abused as a child. Often we grow up thinking that the way we were treated was normal and to be expected when, in fact, it was abusive. Emotional abuse of children includes:

- physical neglect (when a parent does not feed a child or provide the basic necessities such as clothing or shelter, or medical attention if needed)

  Leaving a child alone when he or she is not ready to care for him/herself is neglectful, since it leaves a child in a potentially dangerous situation.

- emotional neglect or deprivation (when parents don't take an interest in their child, and do not talk to or hold and hug the youngster, and are generally emotionally unavailable to the child)

  Alcoholic parents are often neglectful of their children's

needs. Although emotional neglect may not leave physical scars, it has serious consequences for the child.

- abandonment (leaving a child alone in the home or car for long periods of time, not picking a child up at a designated time and place)
- verbal abuse (constantly putting a child down, name-calling, being overly critical)
- boundary violation (not respecting a child's need for privacy, such as walking in on a child in the bathroom without knocking, entering a child's bedroom without knocking, going through a child's private belongings)
- role reversal (when a parent expects his or her child to meet their needs—to, in essence, parent *them*)
- chaotic abuse (being raised in an environment where there is constant upheaval and discord and very little stability)
- social abuse (when parents directly or indirectly interfere with their child's access to his or her peers or fail to teach their child essential social skills)
- intellectual abuse (when a child's thinking is ridiculed or attacked and he or she is not allowed to differ from her parent's point of view)

Emotional abuse is sometimes so innocuous and leaves such invisible scars that many do not realize they were emotionally abused as a child. For this reason, it is important to take the time now to carefully consider the environment in which you were raised and the personalities of those who raised you. For suggestions for further reading on emotional abuse, please refer to Appendix I.

The Effects of Childhood Abuse on Parenting

Although many adults who were abused do not mistreat their children, statistics show that those who were abused as children run a greater risk of becoming abusive toward their children than those who were not abused. If you experienced one or more types of abuse, you are at risk of becoming an abusive parent yourself.

If You Were Physically Abused

Those who were physically abused often become too rough with their children and find that they have to fight the urge to strike them. Or they may suddenly become gripped with rage at what they experience as their child's impudence and strike out uncontrollably. Some even believe that they have the right to physically punish their children as they themselves were punished.

If you have ever experienced moments of uncontrollable rage in which you struck someone, shook someone violently, or pushed someone down, you must assume that this kind of rage is likely to return. And you also must assume that if you were to have children, they might become targets for your anger, since children have the uncanny ability to push their parents' buttons.

Before having a child, I strongly recommend you seek professional help in order to learn the origin of your rage and ways of releasing your anger in constructive ways.

If You Were Sexually Abused

When your first sexual experience is one of manipulation, exploitation, or pain, the effects on your self-esteem and your sexuality can be devastating. One or more experiences with sexual abuse—no matter how minor it seems—causes a child to feel tremendous shame. Since most children blame themselves for the abuse and since most are afraid to tell anyone, their shame stays with them, spilling over into all their future relationships, including their relationship with their children.

If you were sexually abused as a child, there is a very strong possibility that you will either sexually abuse your own children or get involved with partners who are either sexually compulsive, sexually addicted, or sex offenders.

A common pattern for many female survivors is to repeat the cycle of abuse by getting involved with or marrying a child molester who sexually abuses her children, while male survivors are more likely to become sexual abusers. This is because males tend to identify with the perpetrator as a way of avoiding feeling like a victim. Females have also been known to sexually victimize others, of course, but are more likely to reenact their abuse by emotionally or physically abusing their children than by sexually abusing them.

The woman or man who was sexually abused as a child may be appalled at her or his own uncontrollable desire to touch her or his child sexually. Or he may go to the opposite extreme, depriving his child of touch and affection out of fear of being sexual with the child.

In addition, many survivors of child sexual abuse are so frightened that their children will be abused as they were that they become overly cautious, sometimes bordering on paranoia. Examples of extreme behavior are: not allowing their children to walk to and from school alone, even when they have reached an age when it is appropriate, not allowing their children to spend the night at other children's homes or on overnight camping trips, assuming that all males are potential perpetrators and, therefore, never allowing their children to be alone with a male, not allowing their teenage girls to date.

If You Were Emotionally Abused

Those who were emotionally abused as children often end up abusing their own children in the very same way they were abused. Those who were verbally abused or overly criticized are often shocked to hear the same words out of their

mouths that hurt them so much as children: "You're so stu-
pid," "I wish I never had you," and "I hate you."

Those who were smothered or overcontrolled will tend
to repeat the same behavior with their children, even though
they may have vowed to never be like their parents. Those
who were smothered will tend to overinvest in their children,
become emotionally dependent on them, and expect them to
make up for what they lack in their own lives. Those who were
overcontrolled will tend to have unreasonable expectations of
their children and demand total obedience. Many, in an attempt to prevent their children from doing something wrong,
become overly intrusive—not respecting the boundaries and
privacy of their children.

And those who were ignored and deprived by their own
parents will tend to neglect their children, even though they
have no intention of doing so. This occurs for several reasons.
First of all, those who were neglected as children often do not
have the capacity to give to their children what they themselves did not receive. Second, these parents are often so bent
on getting the attention they didn't get as children that they
don't recognize their own children's needs. They are more
likely to expect their children to meet their needs than to meet
their children's needs. And third, some parents who were deprived actually resent their own children's needs and demands
since their own were not met.

The fact that you were abused in any or all of the above
ways does not necessarily mean you shouldn't become a
parent, but it may mean you need to postpone doing so until
you have worked on the attitudes, behaviors, and beliefs that
cause abusive parenting. Experts now know enough about
childhood abuse and abusive parents that we can almost predict who will become abusive and who will not, based not only

on previous abuse experience but on personality characteristics.

Your Family Tree

In addition to exploring your own childhood for signs of abuse or neglect, you will also need to explore your family tree. There are certain behaviors and addictions that run in families, getting passed down from generation to generation, much like a defective gene. Some of these behaviors and addictions are:

- alcoholism and drug addiction
- a tendency toward violent behavior, including the physical abuse of children, spousal abuse, rape, and a history of arrests for violent crimes
- sexual acting out, including the sexual abuse of children, rape, date rape, spousal rape, sexual addictions, and compulsions
- emotional abuse, particularly a tendency to be hypercritical of others and to smother, neglect, or verbally abuse children

If your family has a history of any of the above behaviors or addictions, there is a strong possibility that you are predisposed to the same behavior. Therefore, you need to guard against these tendencies, especially because they will impact the lives of your future children, should you decide to have them. If you have noticed any signs of these behaviors in yourself, I suggest you seek either professional help or participate in an appropriate twelve-step program dealing with the issue (i.e., Alcoholics Anonymous, Narcotics Anonymous, or Parents United) before you decide whether to have a child or not.

In addition, even if you yourself seem to have no tendencies in this direction, you may have developed other coping mechanisms or coping styles that will interfere with you being a good parent. For example, many of those who are children of alcoholics develop what has popularly been called "codependency." This syndrome or way of coping causes people to behave in unhealthy ways, especially in relationship to their partners and children.

Children of alcoholics grow up watching one out-of-control person trying to control another. They get caught up in the needs of both parents and thus become codependents. Codependency is an unconscious addiction to another persons' dysfunctional behavior or a tendency to put other people's needs before your own. Children of alcoholics are robbed of their childhood, since often they are required to take care of their alcoholic parents as well as their siblings and the household. Many adult children of alcoholics are plagued by a sense of failure for not having been able to save their parents from alcohol and some blame themselves for their parents' drinking.

There have been many books written about the issues of codependency and adult children of alcoholics, so I won't go into these syndromes here. Suffice it to say, these issues may interfere with you being as good a parent as you could be.

Recognizing a family pattern of abuse is the first step in eliminating it. Although it may be impossible to eliminate it completely in a lifetime, the goal should be that each generation shows improvement. We have more information available to us about the prevention of child abuse than ever before. There are parenting classes available in most cities, as well as special classes for parents who have been abusive to their children or fear becoming so.

Many people who were abused themselves as children desperately want the opportunity to have children and to provide for them the kind of parenting they didn't get when they were growing up. As much as you have been fearful about perpetuating the abuse you suffered by passing it on to your own child, deep in your heart you probably also feel a desire and a commitment not to pass on the abuse. Through your dedication to the recovery process, you can break the cycle.

The information and questions I've posed in this and the previous chapter are merely a point of departure for more serious soul-searching. There are many books on parenting and child abuse in your public library. The list of recommended books at the end of this book will also provide you with more information on the subject. And any good family therapist or your minister, priest, or rabbi will likely be able to help you sort out your feelings as well.

Some people may tell you that you can think yourself right out of parenthood by worrying about these issues. They will tell you that once the baby has arrived, you will naturally sense how to be a good parent. But what if you don't? What if you bring a child into your life and discover that you are not suited or able to be a good parent? Your child will be the one to suffer the most.

There is no magic to making a decision about parenthood. It takes careful, honest self-appraisal and the willingness to make the decision that is best for you and a potential child. While this is not easy, particularly with the pressures from family, friends, and society to have children, it is the only way you are going to be able to make a decision you can live with for the rest of your life.

Whatever your decision, you can take pride and satisfaction in the knowledge that you have taken the time to carefully think through this important decision. And you are one step closer to being able to either move forward with parenthood or lay it to rest and move on with your life.

ELEVEN

Taking a Close Look
at Your Relationship

ONE OF the most common motivations couples have for
wanting a child comes out of a natural desire to create a child
shared by both, possessing the qualities and characteristics of
both. They want to form a family, to extend the love they
feel toward one another to their offspring. This is a wonderful
reason. But since one out of every two marriages now goes
into decline after a first baby's arrival, it is important to take
a close look at your relationship to make sure you have the
commitment and strength for this to become a reality.

In this chapter, I will help potential parents who are in a
relationship decide whether their *particular* relationship is one
that is conducive to good parenting and to providing a child a
nurturing, consistent, safe environment.

As I discussed thoroughly in Chapter Seven, a new child,
particularly a first child, puts tremendous stress on even the
best relationship. Therefore, if your relationship is already

strained for one reason or another, having a child could cause it to break. But even more important is the effect a strained relationship has on a child: Every child deserves a home where they feel safe and secure. No child should be subjected to chaos, indifference, or bitterness between his or her parents.

You can begin your relationship examination process by answering the questions that follow. Once again, there are no right or wrong responses. The important thing is to answer as honestly as possible.

Questions: You and Your Partner

1. What kind of relationship do you and your partner share? Would you characterize your relationship with your partner as stable, loving, warm, and open or tumultuous, distant, or even cold or bitter?

2. Do you and your partner communicate well or do you have problems in this area? How do you go about resolving conflicts? Is there a problem or disagreement in the relationship that remains unresolved no matter how much you discuss it?

3. How does your partner feel about adding a child to the relationship? Does he or she have any reservations? Have you talked openly and honestly with your partner about the issue? If there are disagreements, how will you resolve them?

4. How much attention do you need from your partner? How much attention does your partner need from you? How much time will a child take out of your relationship with each other? Do you imagine the interaction with a child will enhance your closeness or come between you? (While there is no way to predict the future, personality traits of both partners may provide a clue.)

5. How do you and your partner divide up responsibilities and chores now? How will you share the additional work of raising a child? If one of you feels unduly burdened by the extra workload, how will you resolve the problem?

6. What are your financial resources? Could you support a child if only one of you worked? Are you comfortable with the idea of day care? Are you willing to lower your accustomed standard of living?

7. Do you agree on the basics of religion? Discipline? Values? Goals?

8. What kinds of contingency plans are you willing to make in case you are separated after a child enters your life, either through death or divorce?

9. Does your partner have any children from a previous relationship? If yes, what effect might these children have on a new child?

Needless to say, there is not enough room in this book to tackle each issue a couple will discuss as they decide whether or not to become parents. In my practice, however, I have found the following areas bear close examination prior to introducing a child into a relationship: whether you currently communicate well with your partner, what the current balance of power is in your relationship, how jealousy and possessiveness are currently manifested in your relationship, what role models each of you had for relationships, whether you are in agreement over issues such as how to discipline a child, and whether or not one or both of you has a tendency toward substance abuse. In the following pages, you will have the opportunity to consider each of these issues. Once you and your partner have addressed the questions which follow, set aside time to discuss your answers.

Do You Have Good Communication Between You?

One of the most important areas of your relationship to examine is how you communicate with one another, as the ability to communicate well is the cornerstone of any relationship. This becomes even more important when it is time to come to agreements (or compromises) about such potentially volatile subjects as discipline, dependency, or the division of labor once your baby is born. In order to evaluate the level of communication in your relationship, please answer the following questions as honestly as you can:

1. Do you feel your partner listens to your point of view when you disagree or do you get the feeling that he or she is too busy arguing with you?

2. Do you feel you listen to your partner's point of view or are you too busy thinking of what you are going to say to counter his or her remark to really listen?

3. Does it make you feel so uncomfortable to have your partner disagree with you that you tend to run an issue to the ground, trying to make your partner see your point of view?

4. How about your partner? Is he or she ever willing to agree to disagree?

5. Do you feel you fight fair? Or do you pull out all the stops and begin to name-call, insult your partner's intelligence, or threaten to leave the relationship?

6. How about your partner? Does he or she fight fair or become insulting or threatening?

7. Do you use "I" statements when communicating your grievances to your partner, such as "I need you to listen to me"? Or do you use "you" statements, such as "You never listen to me."

8. How about your partner? Does he or she generally use "I" statements or "you" statements?

9. Do you tend to communicate to your partner about issues that are bothering you as they come up or do you tend to store them up until you explode?

10. How about your partner? Does he or she communi-

cate openly about issues in a timely fashion, letting you know when things bother him or her or wait until he or she has reached the boiling point?

If it seems apparent to you from answering these questions that you and your partner have problems with communication, I strongly suggest you enter couples therapy or marriage counseling for even a few sessions in order to learn how to communicate with one another more effectively before you bring a child into your relationship. A good couples' counselor will be able to point out the mistakes you are making in your communication and teach you more effective methods.

Is There a Balance of Power in Your Relationship?

Healthy relationships are made up of equals. This means that both parties contribute equally to the relationship and that each is seen as an equal in the other's eyes. On the other hand, unhealthy relationships demonstrate an inequality of power created because one person feels superior to the other.

Up to now, you and your partner may have settled into a rather comfortable and familiar way of dealing with one another. This does not mean, however, that your way of relating has necessarily been as healthy as it could be.

Prior to adding a child to the relationship mix, it is important to check your current balance of power. Answering the questions below can help you spot any inequality that exists. Take some time to think seriously about the questions before you answer them.

• Who has the most personal power in the relationship—you or your partner? By "personal power," I mean who do you feel is the stronger of the two (in terms of being able to ask for what you want, being able to take care of yourself emotionally)?

- Who usually gets his or her way in choosing what you will do at any given time? Who has control over the finances? Who is most in control in your sexual relationship?
- Which one of you is the most successful in your career? Who makes the most money?
- Which one of you has the most self-confidence? Which one feels the best about himself or herself?
- Who would you say feels superior to the other in the relationship?
- Which one of you seems to be the least satisfied with your partner and with the relationship? Which one has the most complaints about not getting your needs met? Which one is the most critical of the other?
- Who would you say loves the other the most? Who is the most emotionally dependent on the other? Which one of you would have the hardest time going on without the other one?

If the answer to most of these questions was "me," you have the most power in the relationship and therefore probably control the relationship far more than your partner does. On the other hand, if you answered "my partner" to most of these questions, your partner has the most power.

If You Tend to Have More Power in Relationships

If you've answered "me" to most of these questions, it is important for you to ask yourself how you are handling the power you have in relation to your partner. Also, did you choose your partner in the first place so you could feel powerful and in control? This was the situation with Ivan:

"I realize now, much to my dismay, that I chose to get involved with Teddy in the first place because she seemed so weak and helpless. Being around her made me feel great because it made me feel so much stronger than I really am. I was the strong one in the relationship; I was the one in charge for a change. Unfortunately, I didn't realize that I would begin to hate her for her weakness, just as I hate myself for my own. Once I was in the position of power, I slowly began to misuse that power by demanding more and more from her and by becoming more and more critical. In the meantime, I wasn't dealing with my own weaknesses and problems but compounding them because I was liking myself less and less the more abusive I became."

The Price of Tyranny

Whenever you try to control another person, you are taking a tremendous risk—that the person you are controlling is going to resent you and eventually become enraged with you. Tyranny always has a price, either because the person you tyrannize will eventually rebel and retaliate or because you will eventually come to hate yourself for using your power over someone.

The Price of Passivity

It is as destructive to both you and your relationships to allow someone to dominate you as it is to be the one who is dominated. When you get involved with someone whom you perceive as being "better" than you are in some way—either because they seem more intelligent, stronger, more successful, more attractive, or more powerful—you are setting yourself up to be controlled by that person.

If you do have an imbalance of power in your relationship, you will need to work toward creating more balance before you have a child. Otherwise, your child will get drawn into your power struggles, feeling like he or she must side with one or the other of you. In addition, you will be modeling to your child that in every relationship there is a dominate person and a passive person, a victimizer and a victim.

Jealousy and Possessiveness

As discussed in Chapter Seven, often a new baby doesn't bring a couple closer together as much as create new stresses in a relationship and accentuate those problems that already existed. For example, if one or both of you already have a tendency to feel jealous or possessive of your partner, the arrival of a new baby will more than likely stir up these feelings inside you. If one of you already feels neglected by the other because you feel your partner doesn't spend enough time with you, bringing a new person into the relationship will likely exacerbate the problem. While there is no way to predict for sure whether one or both of you will become jealous of the time your partner will spend with the baby, the answers to the following questions can be good indicators.

1. Do you feel your partner doesn't spend enough time with you?

2. Do you feel jealous or threatened by the time and attention your partner spends with his/her job or career? How about his/her hobbies or other activities?

3. Do you feel jealous or threatened by your partner's friends or by the time he or she spends with friends?

4. How about the time your partner spends with family?

5. Do you feel jealous or threatened by your partner's previous relationships?

6. Do you often complain because your partner spends too much time watching TV and not enough time paying attention to you?

7. Do you fear a child will take away even more of your partner's time and attention?

8. Do you feel you might become jealous or threatened by your partner's attention to your child?

9. Do you want a child because you feel neglected by your mate?

If you answered yes to more than two of the above questions or if your partner did, I would suggest you work on your relationship further before considering having a child, perhaps by seeking outside help. If you are already feeling neglected by your partner or jealous of the time he or she spends with others, the chances are high that you will also resent the time your partner spends with your child. This is especially true for males, since new mothers become so consumed by their new child that they do tend to neglect their partner.

Some women who feel neglected by their partner erroneously think that if they have a baby to keep them company, it will make up for the attention they do not get from their partner. But that situation often creates an unhealthy relationship between parent and child where the child is expected to meet the needs of the parent—instead of the other way around. Also, ironically, sometimes a neglectful partner will become so enthralled with the new baby that he ends up spending even less time with his mate.

Still another thing to consider if either you or your partner exhibits jealous or possessive behavior is that for some, no matter how much attention they receive from their partner, it is never enough. This is because the problem lies inside of themselves, not in the relationship. A person who requires the undivided attention of their mate suffers from problems of low self-esteem and insecurity caused by their own upbringing—something which has little if anything to do with the relationship itself or the behavior of their partner. If this is your situation, not only will a child create still further problems in your relationship (since your partner will once again be paying attention to someone other than you), but you may inevitably become jealous and possessive of your child as well.

Did You Have Good Role Models?

Just as it was important to examine the way your parents treated you as a child, it is equally important to take a close look at the way they treated one another. Their relationship taught you important messages about communication, trust, intimacy, and respecting others. If you and your partner are having problems with communication, looking at the patterns you were raised with and reconciling different approaches to handling stress can help make your communication more effective.

1. Describe your parents' relationship. Was it open? Loving? Or distant? Full of anger?

2. Do you feel your parents really loved one another? Were they openly affectionate with one another?

3. Did your parents seem to communicate well with one another, to be able to reach a compromise?

4. How often did your parents argue? What did they argue about?

5. How did your parents resolve conflicts between themselves? Did they argue, talk things over rationally, or ignore conflicts altogether?

6. Did your parents ever stop talking to one another for long periods of time?

7. Did one parent often threaten to leave the other when they fought?

8. Did one parent ever leave the house during an argument?

9. Did their arguments ever turn into yelling and screaming, or physical violence?

10. Did your parents ever separate?

If your parents were not good role models, you and your partner may have more work to do in terms of knowing how to relate to one another in healthy ways. This may include looking for healthier role models and learning healthier ways of relating to one another before bringing a child into the relationship.

Are You in Agreement About Discipline and Dependency?

Differences in family background and personality can create considerable conflicts after a first baby is born. No matter how much they love each other, no two people share the exact same values or feelings or have the same perspective on life and few things highlight these personal differences as pointedly as the birth of a child.

Consequently, an important aspect of your relationship to examine closely is whether you and your partner are in agreement about some basic aspects of parenting. Disagreements about child-rearing tend to center around two issues: discipline and freedom and independence and dependency. For example, some parents feel it is very important for a child to "fit in," to be well-behaved and obedient. Others feel it is more important for a child to be given permission to be independent and unique. Some parents feel it is important not to teach blind obedience and prefer to explain things and reason with their children. Others want instantaneous obedience. If two parents do not agree on these issues, conflicts can ensue that can create a wedge between them and that can confuse their child. Therefore, it is important that you and your partner discuss these issues ahead of time to determine whether you have compatible parenting styles.

This is especially true if you come from vastly different

cultural backgrounds. For example, the age in which adults think children should exercise self-discipline varies widely in different cultures.

Another area of potential conflict is the degree of dependence or independence that can be expected of a child at different ages. In contemporary North America, Britain, and Australia, for example, the emphasis is upon getting through babyhood as quickly as possible and producing an independent child. In many other cultures—Indian and Mediterranean societies, for instance—far less emphasis is placed on independence and the link to the mother is stressed not only for children but for adults too.

Questions: Are Your Discipline Styles Compatible?

1. How were you disciplined as a child?

2. Do you feel this was an appropriate way of disciplining children? Or do you wish to do it differently? If so, why?

3. Are you and your partner in agreement about the purpose of discipline, which methods you will use under what conditions it should be administered and by whom?

4. Do you believe in spanking a child? If yes, under what circumstances?

5. How well do you handle your anger? Do you feel your anger might become a problem when it comes to disciplining a child?

6. Do either one of you have children from a previous relationship? If so, do you agree with the way your partner disciplines his or her children?

7. Do you have a pet? If yes, are you and your partner in agreement on how to discipline your pet? Do you strongly disapprove of the way your partner disciplines the pet or vice versa?

It helps tremendously for couples to talk about their personal beliefs and expectations together. Discuss your differences thoroughly, making certain that each person has a chance to air their feelings. Avoid arguing over who is right and who is wrong but instead ask, "What can we do about this?" Then try to find joint solutions.

Are There Any Indications That Either You or Your Partner Have a Drinking Problem?

Alcoholism affects one out of every ten Americans and there are an estimated twenty-eight million children of alcoholics.

While I cannot tell you whether or not you are an alcoholic (Alcoholics Anonymous has an excellent questionnaire), I can tell you that if you drink excessively or depend on alcohol to reduce stress or "get you through the day," you have a drinking problem and that drinking problem will most certainly negatively affect a child.

The parent who abuses alcohol is emotionally unavailable to his or her children most of the time, especially when drinking. Children of alcoholics (or heavy drinkers) are deprived of love and stability, for it is difficult for them to get their emotional needs met by either the alcohol-abusing parent or their codependent partner. Neither is able to give their child the love he or she needs. In addition, those who abuse alcohol are unpredictable, since they typically undergo an extreme behavior change when they begin to get drunk. Because of the chronic distress in a family where there is heavy drinking, children become hypervigilant, anxious, and chronically afraid.

There is usually little real discipline in a family where there is alcohol abuse. Instead of disciplining a child for misbehaving or in order to help the child improve, parents discipline out of irritation and rage about their own life. Most of the time, it has nothing to do with the child. Without proper discipline, children grow up with poor impulse control, insufficient boundaries, and little willpower. This sets the stage for them to suffer from alcoholism, drug abuse, compulsive overeating, compulsive gambling, and other compulsive and addictive behaviors.

If either you or your partner have a drinking problem, even if you don't consider it alcoholism, you need to get help for the problem before having a child. As mentioned earlier, the stresses of a new child will only exacerbate your present problems and cause you to drink even more. Contact your local Alcoholics Anonymous group or seek professional help from a certified alcohol or drug counselor. Your future child deserves the safety, security, and stability that only sober parents can provide.

Before bringing a child into your relationship, make certain that you have done all you can to resolve your conflicts, establish good communication, and provide a healthy environment for the child. Children need and deserve parents who can provide an environment of stability, consistency, caring, and good communication.

Part V

If You Are Not Ready,
Willing, or Able

TWELVE

Giving Yourself Permission to Wait

IN THIS CHAPTER, I will focus on helping those of you who have discovered that you are either not ready, not willing, or not able at this time to be a good parent. It may have become clear to you or your partner that you need to wait to become a parent or that becoming ready to be a parent will require more than the aid of this book.

Whatever the case, I encourage you to give yourself permission to wait and to view waiting as a positive step, particularly if you have chosen to actively work on becoming better parent material.

By answering the questions I have posed, you may have become aware that you have unresolved issues from your childhood that you need to work on, perhaps through therapy. Or it may have become clear that your partner needs help before he or she will be a good parent.

Waiting also makes good sense when you are unwilling at

this time to endure the stresses and sacrifices of having a child, as was the situation with Barbara and Tom:

"As much as we want a child, Tom and I have decided to wait until he's finished with his residency before having a baby. Tom works such long hours he really wouldn't be any help and he tends to be very irritable, due to lack of sleep. With a new baby in the house, we're afraid we'd both become so cranky that we'd go at each other like cats and dogs. Besides, we need the money I bring in right now and really can't afford me taking any time off."

Another good reason for waiting is when your present lifestyle is not conducive to raising children, as was the case with Gene and Victoria. Both desperately wanted children, but after several sessions of working with me, they both decided against it for the present. A major factor was when we reviewed their childhoods. Gene, who remembered how it felt being a latchkey child, explained it like this:

"I know how lonely it can be to come home to an empty house. Since both Victoria and I work, our children would be alone for several hours after school each night. We live in the city and we don't want our kids playing out in the streets until we get home, nor would it be fair to expect them to stay locked up in the house, especially in the summer when it stays light for so long. All things considered, I think it's best we don't have children unless we move to the suburbs."

Waiting is also a good idea for those of you who are uncertain whether you are willing to make a lifetime commitment to a child. Many have discovered that although they weren't prepared at the time to make such a long-term commitment, they eventually became ready once they either got older, more mature, or less involved with their career. This was the case with Selena:

"When we were first married, my husband John was dead set against having children. It was primarily the responsibility that turned him off. And the idea of making such a long-term commitment. In fact, his friends were surprised that he'd even gotten married. They'd assumed he'd be one of the last of their group to settle down.

"The first few years of our marriage were quite an adjustment for him. I didn't try to possess him but encouraged him to stay close to his friends and continue with his sports and eventually he settled into married life. He started going out with his friends less and wanting to stay at home with me more, working on remodeling the house and taking care of the yard, that kind of thing. Then last year he told me he thought we should start trying to have kids. I was pleasantly surprised, but I didn't make a big deal out of it. I've learned that it works best just to let him come to things on his own. I got pregnant right away and we now have a darling little boy who John adores. Even though he hadn't seen himself in the role of father, he's turning out to be a great one. I'm glad I had the sense to just wait for him to come around instead of pushing."

Waiting to have a baby until an individual or a couple is ready makes good sense in another way as well. More and more people are waiting until they are in their thirties and forties to have their first child and with positive results. For example, the birthrate for unmarried white women between thirty-five and thirty-nine increased by 78 percent from 1980 to 1990 and for those forty to forty-four there has been an increase of 38 percent during the same ten years.

Cassandra came to see me because although she'd reached the age of thirty-seven, she still wasn't ready to have a child. Everyone she knew was telling her that if she waited any longer she probably wouldn't be able to conceive or her baby would be born with a birth defect. In the course of therapy, Cassandra discovered that one of the reasons she wasn't ready to become a mother was that she had unresolved issues about the way her parents had raised her. We worked together for over a year, helping her to release her anger toward her parents and to express the grief and pain of having been abused. Recently, I received a letter from her that went like this:

"Last week I turned forty and discovered, much to my surprise, that I finally feel ready to become a mother. Therapy helped me to get past my anger at my parents but even more so to know that I don't have to be like my parents.

"I'm so glad I didn't let other people pressure me into having a child just because time was running out. As you helped me to recognize, that's not a good reason to have a baby and I wouldn't have been a good parent at the time. Thank you for all your understanding and guidance. I feel confident that one way of another, I'll have my baby, even if I have to adopt."

I was relieved to hear that Cassandra was open to adoption, since women over forty often have difficulty getting pregnant. But with the advances in reproductive medicine, the risks of having a child at an older age have greatly diminished.

Unfortunately, many women and men alike allow the biological clock phenomenon to force them into making a decision about having a child. As they get closer and closer to the cutoff, the pressure to make a choice increases, making them feel as if it's now or never. Many of those who decided to have a child simply because they felt they would miss out on something ended up regretting their decision later on. This is what my friend Lindsey told me:

"I decided to have a baby because I was afraid that if I didn't have one soon, it would never happen. Even though I wasn't sure I really wanted to have one, I was afraid I'd miss out on an important aspect of life if I didn't. Now, looking back, I really wish I'd have waited. I just wasn't ready to be a parent and now it is a real struggle every day. I think if I'd have waited I would have either ended up being a better mother or

I would have decided not to be a parent at all. I'd tell anyone who isn't really sure to wait, no matter how much their biological clock is ticking."

Midlife parents often make very good parents for several reasons. First of all, both men and women often experience a drop in their commitment to work as they reach forty. Jobs and careers often don't hold the same significance as they once did. For this reason, men and women alike begin reconsidering what is important to them and searching for something that will offer some sense of significance and continuity. For many, this search has opened them up to the possibility of having children, as it did with Tracey:

"Ten, even five years ago, my career was enough for me. Now it isn't. I find myself asking the proverbial question: 'Is that all there is?' several times a day. I've accomplished almost all my career goals and it's been wonderful, but I don't want the next ten years to be like the last. I want something more to my life and much to my surprise, I've found myself seriously thinking about having children."

The passage of time also changes many people's feelings about parenthood by altering the way they view themselves. Once a person feels he or she has accomplished what they set out to do in life and sees themselves as a mature adult who is comfortable with herself or himself, having a child can come to be viewed as a positive act instead of a negative one.

Like my client Sunny, many people discover that their changed feelings about parenthood are related more to a sense of maturity than to a chronological age:

"As I've gotten more confidence in myself, I feel more confident about having a child and a desire to share what I've learned and experienced with the next generation. I've grown from being very introverted and shy to being more outgoing and sure of myself and, in the process, my perception of children and parenthood has changed."

Whatever your situation, I suggest you spend more time around children and get a better sense of what parenting is all about. Many people I've talked to tell me that part of their sense of feeling unprepared to become parents was the fact that they knew so little about children and child-rearing. They hadn't been around children in years or even seen many children. Being around babies and toddlers made them feel more comfortable and, for some, more willing to become a parent—as it did with Tatum:

"Children are far less foreign to me now. Several years ago, it was hard for me to even imagine wanting a baby, but now when I think about having a baby, it feels a little more real. I've held lots of them and hung out with them for hours at a time."

Offer to baby-sit your friends' children or become a Big Sister or Big Brother in order to determine just how comfortable you are around children and whether you have the necessary patience, tolerance, flexibility, and ability to put aside your needs.

For Those Who Fear They Will Not Be Good Parents

The reason many of you may still be uncertain about whether or not to become a parent is your fear of making the same mistakes your parents made. While we certainly take on many of our parents' characteristics, attitudes, and beliefs, we are not our parents. For one thing, we have more choices and more information than our parents did. We are fortunate to live in a time and culture that supports parents getting the help they need. Parents are no longer expected to instinctively know how to handle their children and they are not rejected for seeking help. Parent groups, parenting classes, and telephone hotlines are ready, willing, and able to discuss parenting issues. Instead of denying yourself the experience of being a parent because you fear you will repeat your parents' mistakes, discuss your specific fears and concerns with a therapist.

There are many things you can do to lessen your risk of repeating parental patterns or making egregious parenting errors, the first of which is to educate yourself. The more you understand yourself and the dynamics of parenting, the more you can change your dysfunctional attitudes and behaviors.

Today, help is readily available from organizations like Parents Anonymous, which teach parenting skills and stress management in an attempt to help parents and would-be parents. I have listed many of these organizations in Appendix II at the back of the book. In addition, many community colleges teach numerous parenting classes.

As you educate yourself, you will learn to recognize your own strengths and weaknesses and how these will impact a child's development. I have made a list of important points to consider during your education process. Remember, whatever your ultimate decision, any work you do will bear fruit—for greater self-knowledge can only be beneficial to your confidence and happiness. Points to consider:

• Don't have children for the wrong reasons. We are not meant to have children to keep us company, to help us feel less lonely or less empty inside, or to take care of our needs. Nor should we have children to boost our ego, to have someone to control, or to please someone else. Having a child for any of these reasons is setting yourself up to become an abusive parent.

• Parenting is not a popularity contest. Because you will need to provide your children with proper limits, boundaries, and discipline, there will be times when you will temporarily lose your child's affection. If you are not willing to adjust to this, you will bend to your child's wishes in an attempt to maintain his love, risk turning your child into someone who always has to have his way, and thus set yourself up to become enraged with him when he doesn't mind. If you don't feel you could handle your child's rejection or set adequate boundaries and limits, before having a child, you need to find ways of increasing your self-esteem, including entering therapy and finding activities that build your confidence.

- You will need to accept your children for who they are instead of having expectations that are unreasonable or setting goals that are unreachable. You will need to let your child know that you love him or her, no matter what they do, that your love is not predicated on what they do for you, how attractive they are, how popular they are, or how successful they are. If you continue to have a specific image of the child you want to have, if one of your main reasons for wanting a child is predicated on your child achieving what you have not, you need to seriously reconsider parenthood until these fantasies are replaced by more realistic expectations.

- Understand that if you respect your children, they will respect you. Know that respect is not automatically due you, just because you are a parent. You must earn it. The parent who displays no respect for her children can expect little respect in return.

- You will need to teach your children to respect your boundaries and your privacy. You are not doing your child a favor by allowing her or him to intrude upon your space. Instead, you are teaching her or him to be intrusive with others and discouraging her or him from developing a self that is separate from you. If you do not have good personal boundaries, this is something specific you can work on in preparation for becoming a parent.

- You will also need to provide your children with proper discipline and limits. If you are too lenient at times, your child will have a tendency to try to push your limits, which, in turn, will likely cause you to become enraged with him or her. A child who is consistently disciplined knows what to expect and is less likely to push the limits.

- Children need their parents to be affectionate with them, to hug and kiss them, to hold them when they are afraid or need comforting. If you are uncomfortable with such displays of affection, your child will feel deprived, rejected, and unloved. On the other hand, you will need to be careful not to overwhelm your child with too much affection, thus causing him or her to feel smothered and possessed. A child should never be forced or manipulated into being affectionate with his or her parents or put in the position of surrogate mate to a parent.

- Continue to work on yourself and on being a good parent. All parents make mistakes, but it is those who do not recognize when they need help who end up having parenting problems.

For Those Who Were Abused as a Child

All your best intentions, every ounce of your will, cannot stop you from abusing or depriving your child as you yourself were abused or deprived if you haven't worked on your own healing. Unless you have unearthed and ventilated your anger, shame, and fear, you will, perhaps unknowingly, treat your child as you were treated.

Most abusive parents are still angry with their own abusive parents and are acting out this anger with their children. The more you work on releasing your anger in constructive ways, the less likely you will be to abuse your own children.

You must stop downplaying the abuse you suffered and allow yourself to feel and express your anger. Alice Miller, in her wonderful book *For Your Own Good*, describes what happens when we downplay our past abuse:

I have discovered that we are less a prey to . . . the repetition compulsion if we are willing to acknowledge what happened to us, if we do not claim that we were mistreated "for our own good," and if we have not had to ward off completely our painful reactions to the past. The more we idealize the past, however, and refuse to acknowledge our childhood sufferings, the more we pass them on unconsciously to the next generation.

I strongly recommend either individual or couple therapy if you or your partner were abused as a child. In addition to learning more about how having a history of abuse makes you susceptible to mistreating your children, it will teach you constructive ways of handling stress, better communication and coping skills, and many other tools for more effective parenting, which, in turn, will help you become less frustrated and less likely to abuse your children.

I also suggest you join a support group, for several reasons. First of all, it is important to learn to relate more comfortably with other adults in order to develop satisfying relationships and obtain personal support so that you don't need to look to your children for understanding and comfort. In addition, if you have been abused, it is important to realize you are not alone and to work with other parents and potential parents who have the same concerns you do.

Breaking the cycle of abuse starts with you. Every time you take responsibility for your actions, every time you forgive yourself and treat yourself well, you break the cycle of abuse, little by little. Every time you vow to treat your future child with respect and to honor your child's dignity as a human being, you come one step closer to being ready to become a parent.

Staying involved in your recovery program and learning parenting skills will help tremendously. Remember that being a perfect parent is an impossible goal. Raising children is not an easy job, especially today. It requires an incredible amount of tolerance, fortitude, flexibility, adaptability, and support. It requires that you take good care of yourself, that you be completely invested in your recovery so that you can supply the role modeling and limit setting that are necessary aspects of good parenting.

As you recover from your own abuse, you will continually diminish abusive attitudes and behaviors that persist in your present-day experience. Then you can replace the old attitudes and ways of being with viable, nourishing alternatives.

Many who were abused as children become capable, nurturing parents. Sometimes this is because they had a significant person in their lives who modeled good parenting. In other instances, counseling helped them put their pasts into perspective.

Deciding whether or not to become a parent requires clear, realistic thinking, which includes learning the facts about parenthood and being able to realistically assess your parenthood potential. All too often, however, this important decision is based on unrealistic fantasies, misinformation, a lack of awareness about oneself and one's ability to parent.

Whatever your reason for waiting, whether it is to give yourself more time to decide or to give yourself time to make the necessary changes that will ensure you will be a good parent, continue to see waiting as a positive step. While you may feel that you are running out of time, in reality, there is no such thing. If and when you decide to become a parent, there will be a way and the time for you to do so.

Waiting to have a child when you desperately want one *now* can be agonizing. Therefore, those of you who have decided to wait in order to work on yourself, your relationship, or the environment into which you will bring your child should be commended. You have placed the needs and welfare of your future child ahead of your own immediate needs and this in itself shows that you have the potential to be an excellent parent.

THIRTEEN

Giving Yourself Permission to Be Childfree

SOME OF YOU may now be clear that parenthood is not for you. You may have decided that your lifestyle is not conducive to parenting or that you have other priorities and goals that are more important to you. For you, this decision probably brings some sadness, but it may bring more relief than pain.

Others, however, have realized, in the course of reading this book, that it would be best if they didn't become a parent because they believe they lack what it takes to be a good one. If this is the case, I applaud your integrity and sympathize with the difficulty of such a decision. I have nothing but respect for those of you who have honestly assessed the situation and determined that because of your personality, your childhood background, the status of your relationship, or a combination of factors, you would be unsuited for parenthood and would, in fact, be doing some child a great favor by not becoming a parent.

You are not alone but among a growing number of thoughtful, mature, caring, forward-thinking people who have decided to remain childless. There are more childless adults in America right now than in any other time in our history. Nearly 20 percent of women in the baby boomer generation are not having children, according to U.S. census takers.

One example of such a person is Oprah Winfrey. During the taping of a show that aired in April of 1984, Oprah said she was not willing to make the sacrifices necessary to be a parent, nor did she have sufficient patience to be a good parent. She told her audience that at that time she was under a great deal of pressure from friends and fans alike to have a baby but that even though she had enough money and resources to have a child and bring it to work with her, she believed it would not be fair to the child.

Oprah had obviously carefully weighed the pros and cons of becoming a parent and determined that since she could not be the kind of parent she wanted to be, she'd forgo parenthood.

Many others have decided to forego parenthood for the same or similar reasons. Melinda felt it would be unfair to expect a child to conform to her lifestyle:

"My days are extremely hectic. I rarely get home before 8 P.M. and when I do, I'm exhausted. I could afford a full-time nanny, but then it would be she who was raising my child, not me."

Of all the attributes necessary for motherhood, patience is the one in which voluntarily childless women most often feel deficient. As Suzanne, a previous client of mind, stated:

"Being a good mother means you have infinite patience and devotion to a little helpless creature who needs you desperately and deserves your time. Unfortunately, that doesn't describe me."

Others have more personal reasons for forgoing parenthood. Erica found after several sessions with me that her ambivalence about becoming a mother centered around her fear that taking care of a child's needs and demands would obliterate her hard-won identity:

"I have a history of giving myself away in relationships. A child takes so much time and energy that I'm afraid of losing myself, afraid that I wouldn't be able to maintain proper boundaries and my own needs would be ignored."

Carmen too feared having a child would be a continuation of her past, a past she desperately longed to be free of:

"I took care of other people's needs all my life, starting when I was a small child. My mother died when I was eight and I was expected to cook for my father and to raise my brothers and sisters.

"When my youngest sister got married, I finally felt free—for the first time I could remember. I moved out and got a job and went to school at night and I loved my freedom. But then I met Tony and we got married. It all happened so fast we didn't have time to talk about things like whether we wanted to have children or not. All we knew was that we loved each other desperately and wanted to be together.

"We were married for three wonderful years before we seriously began talking about having children and it was because our families began pressuring us. Tony was shocked when I told him I didn't want to have children. He'd just assumed we eventually would. But when I explained to him how I felt like I'd already raised a family and how much I needed my freedom, he finally came around. Going against our families' expectations and our Hispanic cultural tradition has been difficult, but they see how happy Tony and I are with our lives and I think they'll eventually come around too."

Still others realized that they were too perfectionistic to be good parents. They didn't want to risk imposing their unrealistic expectations and standards on a child, as many of their own parents did. This was the case with Veronica:

"I'm such a perfectionist that I'm afraid I'd become as critical as my mother was with me. Also, because of her criticism and insistence on perfection, I'm very self-critical and I know I'd expect myself to be a perfect mother, which, of course, I can't be. I'm afraid I'd just be too demanding and I don't want to pass that stuff on."

Often couples come to the conclusion that it is important for both parents to want a child and that since one is ambivalent or neutral about the idea, it is best they forgo parenthood.

Still other couples decide to remain childfree because one of them lacks the qualities necessary to be a good parent, as it was with Gordon and Faith:

"Gordon would make a terrific father, since he's patient and he loves kids. But with my high-strung personality, we've agreed that for us, a family isn't feasible. We've opted instead to be my sister's godparents."

I am sure that whatever your reasons are for choosing to remain childless they are valid ones, based on a tremendous amount of thought and infused with much emotion. In this chapter, I will offer you information and encouragement on how you can make the most of your life without children.

Recognizing Your Choices

Language can be extremely powerful, as we all know. Therefore, it's important that you decide what term you wish to use for your status regarding children. Some people prefer the term "childfree" to that of "childless" because the latter connotes a loss of some sort, an incompleteness, a lack or deficiency. On the other hand, some people object to the term "childfree" because it suggests to them that people who do not have children of their own want to be rid of children, as in those who promote a "smoke-free" environment.

For some, including the founder of the ChildFree Network, Leslie LaFayette, "childless" doesn't connote a choice, while "childfree" does. Using the childfree label has helped some people to feel less victimized by the situation, as was the case with Julie:

"I decided I didn't like the 'childless' label. It reminded me too much of the word 'homeless.' After all, I could have had children, but I chose not to. Using the word 'childfree' when I described my situation and correcting others who used 'childless' gave me a feeling of power and I think it made people look at my situation differently, not so much out of pity."

Those who tried and tried in vain to get pregnant also need to recognize that they still have choices, as was the situation with Marjorie and Ted. As Marjorie explained:

"We fought the infertility battle for over eight years. Even though we often felt tired and defeated, we felt as if we had to keep fighting, that we had no other options. We felt like failures because we couldn't get pregnant, because we were infertile.

"Then we decided to attend a group for infertile couples that our doctor recommended to us. When we first heard the people in the group using the term 'childfree,' it sounded ridiculous to us; after all, we didn't feel 'free' at all. We felt trapped in the infertility merry-go-round. And we still desperately wanted a child. But gradually, after talking to other couples, it became clearer to us that we did have an *option* to live childfree instead of continuing to struggle to have a baby when it was clear it wasn't going to happen. It's amazing how using that term made a profound difference in our attitude. We began to recognize that we had made a choice—we could stop our treatments and accept that we weren't going to have a child."

Some people, like Marjorie and Ted, choose not to have children at all if they can't get pregnant. If this is the case with you, it is still important to recognize that being childfree is a choice you made, since you could have a child through adoption. The point is, no one needs to live a childfree life today unless they choose to do so.

Regrets and Second-Guessing

A critical part of deciding to live childfree includes putting to rest for good the ghost of second-guessing: "Should we have?" "Could I have?" "Did I make a mistake?"

Don't waste hours or days or years berating yourself for somehow missing the boat, for not having the family everyone else has, or comparing your life to your fantasy life filled with perfect children.

The first thing you must come to terms with is just what you imagine you are missing out on. One of the most commonly asked questions of childfree adults and one of the questions they ask themselves when contemplating a childfree lifestyle, is: "But don't you think you will regret this decision later on in life?"

The best way to address this is to compare your fantasy family with every other family you've ever known, starting with the family you were raised in. Take a close look at your friends' families, the neighbors' families, your siblings' families. You'll soon be reminded of the reality that raising children is not perfect or ideal. It has its moments of warmth and love and intimacy, but it also has its moments of chaos, disappointment, and pain.

It is vitally important to stay in touch with the reality of what you have missed rather than the fantasy. You may not be able to avoid feelings of loss and regret when you see a mother with a baby in her arms or a father walking with his arm around the shoulder of his ten-year-old son, but you can find ways of coping with these times of regret, such as reminding yourself of all you have achieved and accomplished as a result of your decision.

Second-guessing ourselves and wondering what might have been is the most human of foibles. But believe me, there are far more parents who have regrets about the kind of parents they were or who have second thoughts and regrets about their decision to parent in the first place, than there are people who chose to remain childless. Whenever you start to second-guess about your decision, ask yourself: "Which would I rather have regrets about: *not* having children or *having* them?"

The Positives of Being Childfree

Often people don't realize that many of the good things in their life are possible *because* they are childfree. The next time you begin to think about all the things you're missing out on by not being a parent, do the following exercise:

1. Make a list of all the positive things you have going for you in your life.
2. Take a good long look at your list and think about which of the items you've listed would not be possible if you had a child.

If your life is full of benefits because you are childfree, be grateful for them and begin to take advantage of them. If you can't think of the benefits of being childfree, the following list may remind you:

• personal freedom to come and go as you wish
• more energy to devote to your mate, therefore a closer, more intimate relationship with your mate

- more time and energy for your career
- more energy to devote to a particular sport, artistic endeavor, or avocation
- more money and time to spend on traveling
- more money with which to live more comfortably
- more time and energy to devote to self-improvement or education

There are infinite ways to lead a meaningful, successful life other than by becoming a parent. Childfree living need not be merely tolerated but can be a positive, fulfilling, and joyous experience.

Finding Alternatives to Parenthood

Another way to combat regrets and second-guessing is to incorporate children into your life in other ways. Even though you have chosen to not have your own child, you can still have meaningful relationships with children. Below are some suggestions for how to make children a part of your life.

- Act a godparent or "aunt" or "uncle" to your friends' children. Make a point of seeing the child on a regular basis, taking him or her to the park, to the movies, or to the beach.
- Offer yourself as caretaker for your friends' and family members' children. Offer to baby-sit on a regular basis, help plan birthday parties and other events.
- Become a foster parent.
- Become a Big Sister or Big Brother.
- Become a mentor.
- Befriend a child in your neighborhood.
- Tutor kids at the library after school.
- Volunteer in hospitals to care for sick children.
- Become a scout leader.
- Lead a Boys Club or Girls Club.

• Teach Sunday school.

There are millions of children who would benefit enormously from the involvement in their lives of one caring adult. Children desperately need adults in their lives and they look to them for a variety of important things, including: attention, support, appreciation, role-modeling, and setting limits. You don't have to look far to find a child who will benefit from your attention, and you can never underestimate the impact this can have on the life of a child.

Shaping a Successful Social Life

Shaping a successful social life can be particularly difficult if you are surrounded by couples and singles with children. For example, friendships with those who have children can become strained or broken because it may seem that you no longer have much in common. Parents, especially new ones, have a need to talk about their children and their experiences and feelings about being a parent. Most friendships are built on common interests and when these interests change it can weaken or put a strain on the relationship. This is what happened with Loni and her friend Wendy:

"Wendy and I were close friends for over ten years. We had so much in common, like the fact that we were both teachers and our mutual interest in writing children's books. Then Wendy had her first child and things began to change. At first, I didn't notice it so much; we still saw each other frequently, although mostly it was me going to see her at her house instead of our lunches out. I adored her son Chad and I was so thrilled to see her happy that I didn't mind that we talked mostly about what cute or wonderful things Chad did.

"Then she had her second child, Carly, and things really changed. We saw each other less often and she stopped calling me on the phone. Whenever I called her, it was always obvious that she was preoccupied with the kids. She still asked me about what was going on with me, but I could tell she was just doing it to be polite and wasn't really interested. Soon I began to feel like it was an imposition for her to take the time to talk to me, so I gradually stopped calling.

"After nearly six months, she called me in order to ask me a professional question, acting like nothing had happened between us. When I finally confronted her about not calling me, she apologized but then got defensive, saying that because I didn't have children of my own, I couldn't possibly understand how difficult it was for busy mothers to keep up with friendships. We haven't talked since."

Like Wendy and Loni, many friends drift apart when one has children and the other remains childless. There is sometimes a subtle yet pervasive tendency of new parents to condescend to those who have not yet experienced the joys of pregnancy, birth, or tending to small children or babies. Spoken and unspoken statements, like: "You couldn't possibly understand, since you haven't had children of your own," "Your life just isn't as fulfilled as mine because you don't have children," and "I feel sorry for you; you just don't know what you're missing" can make those who are childfree feel angry, alienated, or, worse yet, inadequate.

All of the above comments have a common thread: They are condescending in tone and content and serve to raise the person who is a parent to a position of superior experience, knowledge, or morality from that of the childless adult. Sometimes such comments are meant to hurt you and sometimes they are simply thoughtless and careless remarks. Whatever the case, you will be able to cope with and address them best once you recognize the motivation behind them. The most important thing, however, is not to be intimidated by them.

Another problem that often occurs between those who

have children and those who don't is the misconception that those who remain childfree don't like children. Emily and Jeff were hurt when their longtime friends Caroline and Todd didn't invite them to their regular Fourth of July party. After agonizing over it for quite some time, they decided to ask their friends for their reason. After a few embarrassing moments of silence, Todd said, "Well, to tell you the truth, we didn't invite you because everyone was going to be bringing their children." While most people make these decisions and remarks due to ignorance, not malice, they can be painful nevertheless.

Strong, supportive, loving friendships are crucial to our well-being, but most particularly to those of us who remain single or childless, those who need to create their own families from friends. If you are still close to your friends who have children, then you can work to become an integral part of their children's lives, as mentioned earlier. But if you have found that your friendship has become strained or weakened by the fact that you are childless, it may be time to pursue friends who are also childfree. Seek out those who are living happy and positive childfree lives and get to know them. In order to find such friends, become involved in activities that appeal to adults whose lives are not child-centered, such as adult discussion groups, travel clubs, and so on. Let people know you are looking to meet others who are childfree. Ask coworkers if they know anyone who is childfree and if they do, ask them if they will invite both of you to have coffee or a drink after work.

Once you have met some kindred spirits, you may want to set up an informal network in which you keep in touch, plan occasional get-togethers or share information.

In addition, the ChildFree Network has over fifty chapters throughout the United States and there may be one near you. The organization is based on the following beliefs:

• That childless adults, whether they are childless by choice or chance, have a right to be recognized, respected, and appreciated for their unique contributions and not to be judged on whether or not they have children.

- That too many people are not giving enough careful thought to the decision to have children in this country today.
- That it is time to begin to honestly educate our young people to the realities of parenting.
- That biology is not destiny, that one's self-esteem and sexual identity should have nothing to do with one's fertility or virility.
- That we are whole and complete just the way we are.
- Once a decision is made not to have children it should be respected by everyone.
- A childfree life can be a full, productive, happy life and should be carefully considered by those who are not absolutely sure they want to be parents.
- It is time our society and our government considers a redefinition of the word "family" to include, rather than exclude, the growing segments of society that do not reflect the traditional families of the fifties.

In the back of Leslie LaFayette's book *Why Don't You Have Kids?*, there is information on how you can form your own ChildFree Chapter. (See Appendix I for more information.)

There are more childless adults in America right now than at any other time in history. According to the U.S. census takers, nearly 20 percent of women in the baby boomer generation are not having children. Therefore, there is no reason you should feel all alone with your childfree lifestyle.

Nor is there any reason for you to feel "less than" or "inferior" to those who choose to become parents. The fact is that parenthood does not suit a sizable minority of people, period.

People are not all the same. Just as thresholds of pain vary from individual to individual, so do a sense of personal boundaries, frustration tolerance, and a need for personal freedom. You have a right to your choice. Be proud of it and grateful for the fact that you had a choice at all. Remember that many, many other people should have made the choice you have made but didn't have the courage or the opportunity.

Bibliography

Belsky, Jay, Ph.D., and John Kelly. *The Transition to Parenthood: How a First Child Changes a Marriage*. New York: Delacorte, 1994.

Engber, Andrea, and Leah Klungness, Ph.D. *The Complete Single Mother*. Holbrook, MA: Adams Publishing, 1995.

Engel, Beverly. *The Right to Innocence: Healing the Trauma of Childhood Sexual Abuse*. New York: Ballantine, 1989.

Genevie, Louis, Ph.D., and Eva Margolies. *The Motherhood Report: How Women Feel About Being Mothers*. New York: Macmillan, 1987.

Lafayette, Leslie. *Why Don't You Have Kids? Living a Full Life Without Parenthood*. New York: Kensington, 1995.

McKaughan, Molly. *The Biological Clock*. New York: Doubleday, 1987.

Pruett, Kyle D., M.D. *The Nurturing Father*. New York: Warner, 1987.

Safer, Jeanne, Ph.D. *Beyond Motherhood: Choosing a Life Without Children*. New York: Pocket, 1996.

Swigart, Jane. *The Myth of the Bad Mother: The Emotional Realities of Mothering*. New York: Doubleday, 1991.

Appendix I:
Recommended Reading

Emotional Readiness for Parenting

Belsky, Jay, Ph.D., and John Kelly. *The Transition to Parenthood*. New York: Delacorte Press, 1994.

Clarke, Jean Illsley, and Connie Dawson. *Growing Up Again: Parenting Ourselves, Parenting Our Children*. New York: HarperCollins/Hazelton, 1989.

Rolfe, Randy Colton. *Adult Children Raising Children: Sparing Your Child from Codependency Without Being Perfect*. Deerfield Beach, FL: Health Communications, 1990.

Swigart, Jane. *The Myth of the Bad Mother: The Emotional Realities of Mothering*. New York: Doubleday, 1991.

Woititz, Janet G. *Healthy Parenting: An Empowering Guide for Adult Children*. New York: Simon & Schuster, 1992.

Parenting–General

Brazelton, Berry T., and Bertrand Cramer. *The Earliest Relationship*. Reading, MA: Addison-Wesley, 1990.

Briggs, Dorothy Corkville. *Your Child's Self-Esteem: Step-by-Step Guidelines for Raising Responsible, Productive, Happy Children*. New York: Dolphin/Doubleday, 1975.

Ehrensaft, Diane. *Parenting Together*. New York: Free Press/Macmillan, 1987.

Elium, Don, and Jeanne Elium. *Raising a Son: Parents and the Making of a Healthy Man*. Hillsboro, OR: Beyond Words Publishing, 1992.

Elium, Jeanne, and Don Elium. *Raising a Daughter: Parents and the Awakening of a Healthy Woman*. Berkeley, CA: Celestial Arts, 1994.

Gurian, Michael. *The Wonder of Boys*. New York: Tarcher/Putnam, 1996.

Nelson, Jane. *Positive Discipline*. New York: Ballantine, 1987.

Pipher, Mary. *Reviving Ophelia*. New York: Grosset/Putnam, 1994.

Single Parenting

Alexander, Shoshana. *In Praise of Single Parents: Mothers and Fathers Embracing the Challenge*. New York: Houghton Mifflin, 1994.

Engber, Andrea, and Leah Klungness, Ph.D. *The Complete Single Mother*. Mass.: Adams Publishing, 1995.

Greif, Geoffrey L. *Single Fathers*. Lexington, MA: Lexington–D. C. Heath, 1985.

Mattes, Jane. *Single Mothers by Choice: A Guidebook for Women Who Are Considering or Have Chosen Motherhood*. New York: Times Books, 1994.

Miller, Naomi, Ph.D. *Single Parents by Choice: A Growing Trend in Family Life*. New York: Insight Books, 1992.

Nelson, Jane, Cheryl Erin, and Carol Delzer. *Positive Discipline for Single Parents*. New York: Prima Publishing, 1990.

Mothering

Bassoff, Evelyn. *Mothers and Daughters: Loving and Letting Go*. New York: Penguin, 1988.

Genevie, Louis, Ph.D., and Eva Margolies. *The Motherhood Report: How Women Feel About Being Mothers*. New York: Macmillan, 1987.

Klein, Carol. *Mothers and Sons*. Boston: Houghton Mifflin, 1984.

Fathering

Coughlin, William. *Her Father's Daughter*. New York: Putnam, 1986.

Helnowitz, Jack, Ph.D. *Pregnant Fathers: Entering Parenthood Together*. San Diego: Parents as Partners Press, 1995.

Louv, Richard. *FatherLove: What We Need, What We Seek, What We Must Create*. New York: Pocket, 1993.

Marone, Nicky. *How to Father a Successful Daughter*. New York: McGraw-Hill, 1988.

Marzollo, Gene. *Fathers and Babies: How Babies Grow and What They Need from You from Birth to Eighteen Months*. New York: HarperCollins, 1993.

Pruett, Kyle. *The Nurturing Father: Journey Toward the Complete Man*. New York: Warner, 1987.

Scull, Charles, ed. *Fathers, Sons, and Daughters: Exploring Fatherhood, Renewing the Bond*. Los Angeles: J. P. Tarcher, 1992. (Contributors include Robert Bly, Bill Cosby, Jack Kornfield, Linda Leonard, Marion Woodman.)

Twilley, Dwight. *Questions from Dad*. Boston: C. E. Tuttle, 1994.

Gay and Lesbian Parenting

Martin, April, Ph.D. *The Lesbian and Gay Parenting Handbook: Creating and Raising Our Families.* New York: HarperPerennial, 1993.

Preventing Abuse

Hart-Rossi, Janie. *Protect Your Child from Sexual Abuse: A Parent's Guide.* Seattle: Parenting Press, 1984.

LeShan, Eda. *When Your Child Drives You Crazy.* New York: St. Martin's, 1985.

Miller, Alice. *For Your Own Good: Hidden Cruelty in Child-Rearing and the Roots of Violence.* New York: Farrar, Straus and Giroux, 1984.

Samalen, Nancy. *Love and Anger: The Parental Dilemma.* New York: Penguin, 1992.

Wyckoff, Jerry L., Ph.D., and Barbara C. Lenell. *How to Discipline Your Six-to Twelve-Year-Old Without Losing Your Mind.* New York: Doubleday, 1991.

Healing Emotional Wounds from Childhood

Beattie, Melody. *Codependent No More.* San Francisco: Harper/Hazelden, 1987.

Black, Claudia. *Children of Alcoholics: As Youngsters–Adolescents–Adults.* New York: Ballantine, 1981.

Bloomfield, Harold H., M.D. *Making Peace with Your Parents.* New York: Ballantine, 1983.

Covitz, Joel. *The Family Curse: Emotional Child Abuse.* Boston: Sigo Press, 1986.

Engel, Beverly. *Divorcing a Parent.* New York: Ballantine, 1990.

———. *The Emotionally Abused Woman.* New York: Ballantine, 1990.

———. *Families in Recovery: Working Together to Heal the Damage of Childhood Sexual Abuse.* Los Angeles: Lowell House, 1994.

———. *Partners in Recovery: How Mates, Lovers, and Other Prosurvivors Can Learn to Support and Cope with Adult Survivors of Childhood Sexual Abuse.* New York: Ballantine, 1992.

———. *The Right to Innocence: Healing the Trauma of Childhood Sexual Abuse.* New York: Ballantine, 1989.

Farmer, Steven. *The Wounded Male.* Los Angeles: Lowell House, 1991.

Leonard, Linda. *The Wounded Woman: Healing the Father–Daughter Relationship.* Athens, OH: Swallow Press, 1982.

Lew, Mike. *Victims No Longer: Men Recovering from Incest and Other Sexual Child Abuse.* New York: HarperCollins, 1990.

Love, Patricia. *The Emotional Incest Syndrome: What to Do When a Parent's Love Rules Your Life.* New York: Bantam, 1990.

Pregnancy

Eisenberg, Arlene, Heidi Eisenberg Murkoff, and Sandee Eisenberg Hathaway, R.N. *What to Expect When You're Expecting.* New York, Workman, 1991 (revised).

Fenlon, Arlene. *Getting Ready for Childbirth: A Guide for Expectant Parents.* Boston, Little Brown & Co. 1986.

Gillespie, Clark. *Your Pregnancy Month by Month.* New York: Harper & Row, 1985.

Jones, Carl. *The Birth Partner's Handbook.* New York: Meadowbrook Press, 1989.

Kitzinger, Sheila. *The Complete Book of Pregnancy and Childbirth.* New York: Alfred Knopf, 1996.

Russell, Keith, and Jennifer Niebyl. *Eastman's Expectant Motherhood.* Boston: Little, Brown & Co. 1989.

Sears, William, and Martha Sears. *The Birth Book.* Boston, Little, Brown & Co., 1994.

Adoption

Arms, Suzanne. *Adoption: A Handful of Hope.* Berkeley, CA: Celestial Arts, 1990.

Gilman, Lois. *The Adoption Resource Book.* New York: HarperCollins, 1992 (3d. ed.).

Mandarin, Hope, ed. *The Handbook for Single Adoptive Parents.* 1992. (Available from Committee for Single Adoptive Parents, P.O. Box 15084, Chevy Chase, MD 20825. Cost: $15, including postage and handling. A must-have book for singles considering or who have chosen adoption.)

Register, Cheri. *Are Those Kids Yours? American Families with Children Adopted from Other Countries.* New York: Free Press/Macmillan, 1991.

The Biological Clock

Bing, Elizabeth, and Libby Colman. *Having a Baby After Thirty.* New York: Bantam, 1980.

McKaughan, Molly. *The Biological Clock.* New York: Penguin, 1989.

Donor Insemination

Baran, Annette, and Reuben Pannor. *Lethal Secrets: The Shocking Consequences and Unsolved Problems of Artifical Insemination.* New York: Warner, 1989.

Noble, Elizabeth. *Having Your Baby by Donor Insemination.* Boston: Houghton Mifflin, 1987.

Robinson, Susan, M.D., and H. F. Pizer. *Having a Baby Without a Man: The Woman's Guide to Alternative Insemination.* New York: Simon & Schuster, 1985.

Childlessness

LaFayette, Leslie. *Why Don't You Have Kids? Living a Full Life Without Parenthood.* New York: Kensington, 1995.

Lisle, Laura. *Without Child: Challenging the Stigma of Childlessness.* New York: Ballantine, 1996.

Safer, Jean, Ph.D. *Beyond Motherhood: Choosing a Life Without Children.* New York: Pocket, 1996.

Mentoring

Freedman, Marc. *The Kindness of Strangers: Adult Mentors, Urban Youth, and the New Voluntarism.* New York: Jossey-Bass/Macmillan, 1993.

Appendix II:
Resources

ORGANIZATIONS

Single Adoption

Adoptive Families of America, Inc.
3333 Highway 100 North
Minneapolis, MN 55422
(612) 535-4829
Provides information on support groups and agencies open to single parents, free information packet. Publishes *Ours: The Magazine of Adoptive Families*, which includes many articles on single parents.

Committee for Single Adoptive Parents
P.O. Box 15084
Chevy Chase, MD 20815
(202) 966-6367
Provides source list and supportive information specifically geared to singles seeking to adopt nationally and internationally.

Families Adopting in Response (FAIR)
P.O. Box 51436
Palo Alto, CA 94306

Provides support for parents of special-needs, transracial, and trans-cultural adoptive children.

Single Parents Adopting Children Everywhere (SPACE)
6 Sunshine Avenue
Natick, MA 01760
(508) 655-5426

Single Parenting

National Association of Single Mothers, Inc. (NOSM)
P.O. Box 68
Midland, NC 28107-0068
(704) 888-KIDS

Ample how-to information for single mothers (and mothering fathers) with emphasis on connecting individuals with local self-help and support groups. Publishes *Single MOTHER* magazine.

Single Mothers by Choice (SMC)
P.O. Box 1642
Gracie Square Station
New York, NY 10028
(212) 988-0993

Provides newsletter, support, and resources for women who choose to be single parents. Support groups in many states and Canada emphasize positive aspects of parenting alone; some local groups also welcome single fathers.

Single Parent Resource Center
141 West 28th Street, Suite 302
New York, NY 10001
(212) 947-0221

Referrals to services and support groups for single parents across the nation; information and materials, including self-help group-development manual.

Sisterhood of Black Single Mothers, Inc.
1360 Fulton Street, Room 413
Brooklyn, NY 11216
(718) 638-0413
A national organization, founded in 1974. Education and support to help black single mothers and their families, including youth awareness projects.

Substance Dependency

Alcoholics Anonymous
Box 459
Grand Central Station
New York, NY 10163
(212) 686-1100

Al-Anon Family Groups
P.O. Box 862
Midtown Station
New York, NY 10018-6106
(212) 302-7240
(800) 344-2666
Fellowship of men, women, and children whose lives have been affected by the compulsive drinking of a family member or friend.

Help for Abusive Parents

Al-Anon/Alateen Family Group Headquarters
P.O. Box 862
Midtown Station
New York, NY 10018
(800) 344-2666
(212) 302-7240

Childhelp/National Child Abuse Hotline
(800) 4-A-Child (422-4453)
For both children and adults; twenty-four-hour crisis, information, and referral number. Trained counselors (with master's degree or higher).

Parents Anonymous
National Office
2230 Hawthorne Boulevard, Suite 208
Torrance, CA 90505
(800) 421-0353
(800) 352-0386 (in California)

Parents United
P.O. Box 952
San Jose, CA 95108
(408) 280-5055
(408) 279-8228 (crisis line)
A nationwide support organization for incestuous families. Provides weekly professional counseling, lay therapy groups, and long-term support where incest has been a factor in family difficulty.

Support for Survivors of Child Sexual Abuse

VOICES in Action
P.O. Box 148309
Chicago, IL 60614
(312) 327-1500
International organization for survivors and their partners (prosurvivors).

Mental Health/Counseling

American Association of Marriage and Family Therapists
1133 15th Street NW, Suite 300

Washington, DC 20005
(800) 374-2638
Send stamped self-addressed envelope for listing of recommended therapists in your area.

American Psychological Association
750 First Street NE
Washington, DC 20002-42422
(202) 336-5500

Depression After Delivery
(212) 295-3994
Support network run by volunteers. Call for information
on postpartum depression, anxiety, and psychosis.

Family Services of America
44 E. 23rd Street
New York, NY 10010
(212) 674-6100
Has agencies nationwide offering counseling services on
a sliding fee scale.

Gay and Lesbian Parenting

Gay and Lesbian Parents Coalition International (GLPCI)
P.O. Box 50360
Washington, DC 20091
(202) 583-8029
Offers information, education, and support. Coalition of
lesbian and gay parenting groups nationwide. Sponsors annual
national conference of lesbian and gay parents and their children. Publishes newsletter for parents and a publication for
children.

Lesbian Mothers' National Defense Fund
Mom's Apple Pie

P.O. Box 21567
Seattle, WA 98111
(206) 325-2643

Provides information and referrals to lesbians currently fighting for their rights as mothers. Also provides a list of support groups and a newsletter.

Gay and Lesbian Adoption

Adoption Information Services
901B East Willow Grove Avenue
Wyndmoor, PA 19118
(215) 233-1380

A counseling and educational service providing comprehensive information about current adoption possibilities. Services offered are specifically helpful to gays and lesbians, including how to locate and work with resources supportive of nontraditional families.

Mentoring/Volunteering

Big Brothers/Big Sisters of America
230 N. 13th Street
Philadelphia, PA 19107
(215) 567-7000

International Youth Council
c/o Parents Without Partners
7910 Woodmont Avenue, Suite 1000
Bethesda, MD 20814
(800) 638-8078

National Rainbow Coalition
1700 K. Street NW
Washington, DC 20006
(202) 728-1180

National program for African American youth, ages eight to eighteen

One to One
2801 M. Street NW
Washington, DC 20007
(202) 338-3844

Information for adults interested in being mentors; programs established in Atlanta, Boston, Long Island, Los Angeles, Newark, New York City, Omaha, Philadelphia, and Richmond.

PERIODICALS

Full-Time Dads

The Journal for Caring Fathers
P.O. Box 577
Cumberland, ME 04021
(207) 829-5260

Includes articles for single fathers and resources for support.

Single Mothers

SingleMOTHER
P.O. Box 68
Midland, NC 28107
(704) 888-KIDS

Call the number above for a free back issue.

Single Mothers by Choice
P.O. Box 1642
New York, NY 10028
(212) 988-0993

Mothering
P.O. Box 1690
Santa Fe, NM 87504
(505) 984-8116

About the Author

Beverly Engel is a noted author, workshop leader, teacher, psychotherapist, and sex therapist. She has over twenty-three years' experience as a marriage, family, child counselor and is the bestselling author of nine nonfiction books, including: *Beyond the Birds and the Bees: Fostering Your Child's Healthy Sexual Development in Today's World; Families in Recovery*; and *The Right to Innocence: Healing the Trauma of Childhood Sexual Abuse.*

She has taught at Antioch University, shared her expertise on *Oprah*, CNN, and other national television and radio programs, and is a frequent keynote speaker at conferences throughout the United States and Canada.